CHALLENGES OF THE
BLACK CHURCH
IN 21ST CENTURY AMERICA

DIFFERENTIAL THOUGHTS AND PERCEPTIONS

CREIGS C. BEVERLY, PHD

AND

OLIVIA D. BEVERLY, PHD

ISBN 978-1-63844-811-2 (paperback)
ISBN 978-1-63844-812-9 (digital)

Christian Faith Publishing, Inc.
832 Park Avenue
Meadville, PA 16335
www.christianfaithpublishing.com

Printed in the United States of America

Contents

FOREWORD

One hundred and twenty-five years ago, through the vision and spiritual groundedness of our forefathers and foremothers, Mount Zion Missionary Baptist rose in Toney, Alabama. It rose out of the corn and cotton fields of difficult times and has maintained itself over the years by generations of congregational believers.

To be sure, the historical legacy of Mount Zion Missionary Baptist Church has not always been easy or, as some would say, not always with "easy sailing." Yet through it all, the common thread holding everything together in the face of contrary winds was and continues to be a deep and abiding faith in our Lord and Savior Jesus Christ.

This deep and abiding faith in our Lord and Savior Jesus Christ is rooted in the unassailable knowledge that Mount Zion is God's church and, as such, will never be allowed through grace to die on the shores of the Red Sea without a way over/through and a way to salvation. It is a living example of what Leonard E. Barrett calls Soul Force (Barrett 1974):

> "Soul force" in "Black talk" describes that quality of life that has enabled Black people to survive the horrors of their diaspora. The experience of slavery, and its later repercussions still remain to be dealt with; and "Soul" signifies the moral and emotional fiber of the Black man that enables him to see his dilemmas clearly and at the same time encourages and sustains him in his struggles. "Force" connotes strength, power, intense effort and a will to live. The combined words—

"soul-force"—describes the racial inheritance of the New World African; it is that which characterizes his lifestyle. (Barrett, Leonard, *Soul-Force: African Heritage in Afro-American Religion*: New York: Anchor Press/Doubleday and Company, Inc., 1974)

This book represents a way and means for Mt. Zion Missionary Baptist Church to continue its historical and current legacy of being a beacon in a world solely in need of navigational direction. To the extent that it provides food for thought and the courage of Black churches to step out on faith, then its purpose and mission will have been realized.

Deacon Willie Leslie

PREFACE

CHALLENGES OF THE BLACK CHURCH IN TWENTY-FIRST-CENTURY AMERICA

Dr. Creigs C. Beverly

The single and perhaps the most important institution over historical time which has enabled people of African descent not only to survive but also to develop has been the Black church. The intent here isn't to minimize the value of other institutions, e.g., the family. It is, however, to suggest that without the Black church as the institutional foundation capable of withstanding contrary and destructive winds, the survival of Black people would have been made manifestly more difficult.

Since the arrival of people of color on the shores of Jamestown, Virginia, in 1619, the struggle not only to survive but to also live with dignity, freedom, justice, and the fundamental rights granted in the US Constitution has been imperfect. This imperfection means that the struggle continues today in twenty-first-century America. The vigilance of an oppressed people and the struggle to break the chains of oppressive systems and institutions must, of necessity, continue.

People of African descent continue to experience disproportionate levels of incarceration; disproportionate high unemployment; undereducation and miseducation; they are the recipients of hatred and abuse from White supremacist groups, economic disenfranchisement, and attempts to roll back hard-fought-for voting rights among other barriers to full emancipation and equality as American citizens.

This book is a call to action for the Black church in the twenty-first century. It is designed to reposition the Black church as the tip of the spear leading to development, transcendence, and of course, spiritual enlightenment. This is necessary, not only for people of color but also for other brothers and sisters who see through eyes differently.

Dr. C. Eric Lincoln, perhaps the nation's premier scholar of the Black church as a social institution, described it as follows (Billingsley and Rodriguez 2007, p. 64):

> Beyond its purely religious function, as critical as that has been, the Black church in its historical role as Lyceum, conservatory, forum, social service center, political academy, and financial institution, has been and is for Black America, the mother of our culture, the champion of our freedom, the hallmark of our civilization. (Lincoln 1986, p. 3)

As so eloquently addressed by Lerone Bennett Jr. (1972) many years ago in his seminal work, *The Challenge of Blackness* :

> Blackness is a challenge because it raises the whole question of values and because it tells us that we must rise now to the level of teaching this profoundly ignorant and profoundly sick society. In order to do that, we must create a new rationality, a new way of seeing, a new way of thinking. Our thinking is and the scholarship which undergirds that thinking is Europe centered, white centered, property and place centered, we see now through a glass whitely, and there can be no more desperate and dangerous task than the task which faces us now of trying to see with our own eyes.

With the Black church at the vanguard of creating the new and qualitatively different for the Black community in the twenty-first century, former setbacks become the predicate for new setups, which form the predicate for comebacks.

ACKNOWLEDGMENTS

The final result of this manuscript is the product of many dedicated persons who have had profound positive effects on the editors' lives. We know that one runs the risk of making unintentional mistakes in pointing out the names of individuals who have influenced and molded their essence. However, a few names must be mentioned. Among these is the wife and coeditor, Dr. Olivia Beverly, who has assisted in all of our endeavors for over thirty years. We must also mention the members of the Mount Zion Missionary Baptist Church, in Toney, Alabama, Wednesday night Bible class, Pastor Ernest Williams, Selma Leslie, and Minister Carolyn Calvin, in particular. We have also been blessed by the personal friendships of Deacons Willie Leslie and Durwood Arrington, Joe Wade and Mitch Cunningham, among others. Both individually and collectively, we thank you all. In addition, we thank all members of the faith-based community who have had a significant influence on our lives.

The Editors

Creigs C. Beverly, PhD

Creigs C. Beverly, PhD, is professor emeritus of social work at Wayne State University in Detroit, Michigan. The recipient of numerous awards and honors, Dr. Beverly was named a Fulbright scholar and professor of sociology and social development at the University of Ghana in West Africa; a fellow at the Center for the Study of African Family Life and Development in Kenya, East Africa; and a Carnegie post-doctorate fellow where he served as a special assistant to Maynard Jackson, the first African American mayor of Atlanta, Georgia.

Dr. Beverly earned his BA degree in sociology and psychology in three years from Morehouse College in Atlanta, Georgia, and an MSW degree from Atlanta University. He earned his PhD at the University of Wisconsin–Milwaukee in urban education with a cognate in urban affairs. He has taught courses in social policy, community organization and development, mental health, alcohol and drug addiction, institutional development, program administration and evaluation, human behavior, and the social environment and research methods.

A nationally respected lecturer, author, and consultant, Dr. Beverly has published over forty-five articles, technical reports, and monographs in areas such as spirituality and African American mental health, social development in the African context, alcoholism in the African American community, international social work, and attributes of progressive social workers.

A frequently invited speaker at state, regional, and national conferences, Dr. Beverly's presentations are noted for their passion, penetrative insights, and application of theory and research to important social and personal problems. A recognized authority in human oppression and idiomatic purposelessness, Dr. Beverly has been quoted in the *Wall Street Journal*, the *Atlanta Journal-Constitution*, the *Carnegie Quarterly*, *National Association of Social Worker News*, the *Detroit Free Press*, the *Huntsville Times*, and the *Christian Science Monitor*, among others. He has also been a frequent guest on various television and radio programs.

Olivia D. Beverly, PhD

Olivia D. Beverly, PhD, is an associate professor at Oakwood University in Huntsville, Alabama. She holds a bachelor of arts degrees in biology and chemistry from then Oakwood College, now Oakwood University, a master's degree in teaching, an education specialist in administration, and a PhD in curriculum and instruction from Wayne State University in Detroit, Michigan.

With over thirty years of experience in the field of education including teaching, administration, curriculum development and implementation, professional development, assessment, evaluations, and consulting, Dr. Beverly has a passion for at-risk students and mentoring African American women interested in pursuing advanced educational degrees.

Dr. Beverly most recently served as the assistant vice president for the division of research and faculty development, the coordinator for faculty development, and the director of the quality enhancement plan at Oakwood University. Additionally, she is an ordained elder and has served in numerous positions within her church.

She is married to the love of her life and the wind beneath her wings—Dr. Creigs Beverly. They have collaborated on numerous projects over the last three decades.

CONTRIBUTORS

1. Dr. Robert Elwood Burns, BS, MDiv, MS, STD, deceased. Dr. Burns had an extensive career in the ministry. He served for thirty-three years as a staff chaplain, senior pastor, and chief of the chaplain service at the West Side Veterans Administration Medical Center in Chicago, Illinois.

2. Willie James Leslie, a lifelong resident of Toney, Alabama, and Madison County. Willie Leslie has been a deacon at Mount Zion Missionary Baptist Church for over fifty years. He is also the designated deacon for new member orientation. When asked what his greatest accomplishment in life was, his reply, "My wife, Callie, two beautiful children, and several healthy grandchildren."

3. Dr. Brye McMillon is a leader, pastor, father, and husband who is concerned with the situation in the Black community today. He uses his position as pastor and community leader to address the cultural, racial, and economic needs of the community. Brye earned a doctor of ministry from Liberty Theological Seminary. He is a thirty-year air force veteran and pastor of Ebenezer MB Church in Athens, Alabama.

4. Mangedwa C. Nyathi, MSW, served as assistant to the pastor and liturgist at the renowned Hartford Memorial Baptist Church in Detroit, Michigan. He was also instrumental in establishing multiple church outreach programs, inclusive of, but not limited to, meals for the elderly and prison visitation trips for children whose parents were incarcerated.

5. Rev. Ernest L. Williams is the senior pastor of the Mount Zion Missionary Baptist Church in Toney, Alabama. He also serves as the mathematics department chair at Calhoun Community College in Decatur, Alabama. He holds a bachelor's degree in mathematics from Alabama State University and a master's degree in mathematics from the University of Pittsburgh. He is currently pursuing a master's degree in biblical studies at Faulkner University. Ernest is married to his lovely wife Veronica. They have three sons. The Williams family resides in Harvest, Alabama.

Social and Historical Roles of the Black Church in America October 1999 Congress of National Black Churches, Inc.

Since its first known beginnings in the early 1700s, the Black church was perhaps the only American social institute owned and controlled by African Americans, a situation that for the most part remains true today. Historically, Black colleges and universities might appear to stand as the exception to this assertion, but as was the case with many prominent American educational institutions, e.g., Harvard University, Black colleges developed largely from religious roots and were often cultivated by religious personalities to serve needs that were religious in their scope and conception. Thus, the relationship between the Black church and Black colleges is an intrinsic association that remains strong even today.

As a social and religious institution, the Black church has served and continues to serve many functions in the lives of African Americans. The list of functions is too vast to treat in substantive detail except in book form, but even a partial list suggests the magnitude of its many roles. Among other functions, the church has served as a place of refuge as well as a vehicle of personal and social betterment; it has provided comfort, support, and direction; it has been a forum for the discussion of community issues wherein group interests could be articulated and collectively defended; it has been the college, as it were, that has educated, trained, and disciplined innumerable African American community leaders who have been active in many fields including politics, law, academics, and civil rights. It has provided the meaningful, universally appealing symbols of hope that have sustained and fueled the vision and resilient group spirit necessary for the social progress of American Blacks. It has been a place in which to observe, participate, and experience the reality of owning and directing an autonomous institution free from the exterior controls of the dominant White society. For these reasons and others, the Black church has served as the organizational hub of African American life (Morris 1984).

What follows is an attempt to discuss, more or less systematically, some of these manifold roles. The order of presentation is roughly chronological, by topic, but is in nowise intended as a complete rendering of the rich and complicated history of the Black church in America.

First Black church and the mutual aid societies

The first Black church on record is the Baptist Church at Silver Bluff, South Carolina, organized sometime around 1724 (Brooks 1922). Other Black churches soon formed especially beginning in the 1790s.

An important note regarding the founding of Black churches is that these congregations were the first self-sustaining groups convened voluntarily and organized and controlled by Blacks. These were the benevolent or mutual aid societies, usually found in cities on the northeastern seaboard region (Mein and Rudwick 1966). In most instances, these benevolent societies were in fact quasi-churches and did not identify themselves as such because their members did not agree on denominational affiliation. Their charters emphasized care of widows and orphans, with stipends to sick members and the provision of education of orphans; they excluded persons of questionable moral character from membership (Tanner 1867).

The first pulpits of those ministers who subsequently provided leadership in the Black church were in the mutual aid societies. Moved by an evangelical commitment and perceiving themselves as called to preach the gospels, the aid societies provided ministers with the pulpits that they had been denied in establishment churches (Jones 1971). The Free African Society in Philadelphia provides an example of this transition from mutual aid society to church. Richard Allen and Absalom Jones organized the society after they were frustrated at their attempts to form a purely religious society. Allen continued to preach, however, and soon the society had forty-two members. When Allen and Jones proposed building a new church, they were opposed, not only by local establishment clergy who "used every insulting and degrading language to try to prevent us from going on" (Allen 1790) but also by influential Blacks. When the growing number of African Americans attending to Allen's preaching became worrisome, he was offered the opportunity to become ordained as an Anglican priest and lead an Anglican congregation. He declined the offer, he said, because he believed the plain and simple Gospel was best suited for his people (Allen 1790).

By 1794, Allen succeeded in opening the Bethel Church, an official part of the Methodist Conference with ministerial oversight from a local White church. After acrimonious debate over property ownership and financial considerations for ministers, a landmark Supreme Court of Pennsylvania decision was found in favor of the Bethel Church, granting it sovereignty in the control of its pulpit and other ecclesiastical affairs. This decision eventually made possible the 1816 founding of the AME Church; thus, Allen and Jones's Bethel Church is regarded as the mother church of the AME Churches worldwide.

The colonization issue

The first national issue confronted by the Black church was the proposed colonization of free Blacks in areas outside of America (Jones 1971). Paul Coffee, a Black sea captain and Quaker, had given impetus to this idea with his successful voyage to Sierra Leone with thirty-eight Black emigrants (Brawley 1937). An American Society for the Colonizing Free People of Color in the United States was organized in 1816, with many officers of the organization being slave owners. Colonization met with strong opposition from Blacks in both the North and South who were convinced that the *de facto* purpose of the organization was the removal of free Blacks which would further discourage manumission and leave slaves even more firmly in the grip of slaveholders (Jones 1971, Simons 1887). A protest to colonization in Philadelphia led by Richard Allen and the Bethel AME Church produced several resolutions, many of them containing propositions that resound with modern arguments on civil justice. The preamble to the resolutions is worth noting for its vision concerning the future of Blacks in America:

> Whereas our ancestors (not of choice) were the first successful cultivators of the winds of American, we their descendants feel ourselves entitled to participate in the blessings of her luxuriant soil, which their blood and sweat manured; and that any measure or system of measures, having a direct tendency to banish us from her bosom, would not only be cruel, but in direct violation of those principles which have been the boast of the republic. (Apthekes 1951)

Nevertheless, some Blacks still felt the only real solution was to remove themselves from the presence of Whites; this alternative remained alive throughout the nineteenth century and is still alive today. The prominent Rev. Lott Carey of Richmond, Virginia, was among the second group of emigrants sponsored by the Colonization Society. Although a man of some status in Richmond, he justified his emigration with reasoning that many Blacks found acceptable:

> I am an African: and in this country, however meritorious my conduct and respectable my character, I cannot receive due credit for either. I wish to go to a country where I shall be estimated by my merits and not by my complexion, and I feel bound to labor for my suffering race. (Lunch 1969)

The antislavery movement

Many Blacks continued to pursue the elusive idea of the beloved community and held true to their hope of the New Jerusalem (Redkey 1969), despite the ever-present obstacle of racism. In pursuit of their dream, some Blacks aligned with Whites that shared their dream in varying degrees. These integrated activities often involved various local and national antislavery and abolition societies (Quarles 1969). The Black church involvement in the antislavery movement is perhaps best personified by the charismatic William Lloyd Garrison who convinced many "free colored brethren" to join him in 1831.

Symbols of hope and freedom

Sociologists who study social movements are in agreement that a shared vision, as evidenced by slogans and shared metaphors for understanding and creating social reality, is the essential component of a successful social movement. In this domain, the Black church has all along reigned supreme. No other American institution can claim to have contributed so much to the creation and dissemination of sustaining symbols that made possible the progress of Blacks in America.

In this vein, theologian Lawrence N. Jones has described a widely shared dream of many Black churchmen in nineteenth-century America (Lincoln 1974). They dreamt of a new day whereupon all people would enjoy the full benefits of citizenship as defined in the Declaration of Independence. The primary faith of many nineteenth-century churchmen was the deeply held conviction of sovereignty, righteousness, justice, and the mercy of God. They looked forward to the New Jerusalem—the City of God—where these godly attributes would be accessible to all, just as did the early pilgrims and other immigrants coming to America (Johnson 1999). The churchmen hoped for the actualization of ideals rooted in the Declaration of Independence and the Constitution and dreamed that one day would arise an earthly community in which Blacks would be citizens with all the rights, prerogatives, and responsibilities afforded Whites.

Another important aspect of the symbolizing functions of the Black church is found in music and prayer. One of the greatest sources of strength in the darkness of bondage was sacred music that brought light, support, and powerful inspiration (Work 1915).

Urbanization and social migration

The great rural-to-urban migration of the Black population between 1910 and 1960 brought about a correspondingly tremendous growth in the urban church. The growth was such that Mays and Nicholson raised the question of whether Blacks were "overchurched." The question stemmed from their findings in Atlanta where Blacks comprised 33 percent of the total population but owned 57.5 percent of the churches and in Birmingham where Blacks comprised 33 percent of the population, yet 53 percent of the churches were Black (Mays and Nicholson 1933, p. 209). As with its rural counterpart, the urban Black church continued to provide comfort and escape from racism and social hostility—and escape that became even more important due to the stresses of urban life.

The civil rights movement and current social trends

The great south-to-north migration made it possible for the urban church to function on a larger scale compared with those in rural settings. With mass populations, some churches became organizations of considerable power. These churches not only served as organizational centers for the Black masses, they also commanded allegiance.

The "soul" of the Civil Rights Movement (1950–1984) was beyond question the Black church. The movement's prominent leadership comprises a roll of Black church and religious leaders that included Drs. Martin Luther King Jr., Ralph Abernathy, Wyatt T. Walker, C. T. Vivian, William Jones, Charles Adams, Benjamin Mayes, and others (Washington 1964, p. 292). Before the Civil Rights Movement, there was the Liberation Ministry of the Black church. The AME Zion Church, from its beginning, was dubbed "the freedom church" with links and associations with the following well-known Black Americans: Frederick Douglas, Harriet Tubman, Sojourner Truth, Joseph Charles Price, and James W. Wood (Marshall 1970).

It should also be noted that Black colleges, another prominent African American institution, have been intertwined with the goals and objectives of the Black church. The developmental trajectories of Black leaders and preachers have been such that many presidents of Black colleges have also been ministers or pastors of Black churches.

The social organization of the Black church

Dr. Allen Morris makes the case that the institution of the Black church, although a complex organization, is not a bureaucratic organization. The church is indeed organized but not in a highly formalized way. Unlike a typical bureaucracy, the personalities of the ministers play a central role in the structuring of church activities. A major organizational feature is the loyalty and commitment of church members toward the minister. This contrasts with traditional bureaucracy where personalities tend to be discouraged and formal rules and structured job descriptions take their place. The Roman Catholic Church served as the case study upon which these classic sociological descriptions of bureaucracy as an organizational form were based (Weber 1958). The relationship in the Black church between ministers and church members is characterized as *charismatic leadership*. Under this leadership style, the personality of the preacher is projected throughout the organization; the preacher presides over the church and is ultimately responsible for the overall functioning of its committees and groups. Thus, in the words of W. E. B. Dubois, "The preacher is sure to be a person of executive ability, a leader of people, and a shrewd and affable president of a large and intricate corporation" (Dubois 1899/1967, p. 197). This is a very vital and responsive form of organization. The minister, more than anyone else, often determines the goals of the church and the causes supported by the congregation. The social power of the minister stems from considerable control over the collective resources of the church and personal persuasiveness (Morris 1984).

Church History References

Allen, Richard. 1790. *The Life, Experience, and Gospel Labors of the Right Rev. Richard Allen*. Philadelphia, pp 14–16.

Aptheker, Hertbert. 1951. *A Documentary History of the Negro People in the United States*. New York: The Citadel Press. Vol. 1, pp. 71–72.

Brawley, Benjamin. 1937. *Negro Builders and Heroes*. Chapel Hill: The University of North Carolina Press, pp 35–40.

Brooks, Walter H. 1922. "The Priority of the Silver Bluff Church and Its Promoters." *Journal of Negro History*, Vol. 1H, No. 2, pp. 172–174.

Burns, Robert E. 1975. Doctoral dissertation. "A Study of Effective Preaching from an Analysis of the Preaching of Henry Ward Beecher." Garrett-Evangelical Theological Seminary at Northwestern University, Evanston, Illinois.

Carter, Harold A. 1976. *The Prayer Tradition of Black People*. Valley Forge: Judson Press, pp. 19–20.

DuBois, W. E. B. 1899. *The Philadelphia Negro*. New York: Schocken Books, pp 197–207. (Second Printing in 1967).

Giddings, Paula. 1984. *Then, When and Where I Enter*. New York City: William Morris and Company, Inc.

Hughes, Langston and Arna Bontemps (Editors). 1949. "Let America Be America Again" in the *Poetry of the Negro*, 1746–1949. New York: Doubleday and Company, Inc., pp. 106–108.

Jones, Lawrence. 1971. "They Sought a City: The Black Church and Churchmen in the Nineteenth Century." Union Theological Seminary Quarterly Review. New York, pp. 253–255, 257–258.

Lincoln, C. Eric. 1974. (Editor). *The Black Experience in Religion*. New York: Anchor Books, pp 6, 65–139.

Lynch, Hollis R. 1996. "Pan-Negro Nationalism in the New World before 1862."

Marshall, Calvin B. 1970. "The Black Church: Its Mission Is Liberation." *The Black Scholar*. Vol. 2., No. 4, pp. 13–19.

Mays, Benjamin E. 1968. *The Negro's God*. New York: Atheneum, p. 46.

Meier, August, and Elliott M. Rudwick. 1966. *From Plantation to Ghetto*. New York: Hill and Wang, pp 88–90.

———. 1966. *From Plantation to Ghetto*. New York: Atheneum.

———. *The Making of Black America*. New York. Vol. 1. p. 48.

Morris, Aldon D. 1984. *The Origins of the Civil Rights Movement*. New York: The Free Press, p. 5.

Payne, Daniel A. 1984. *A History of the African Methodist Episcopal Church (1816–1866)*. Nashville Publishing House of the AME Sunday School Union.

Quarles, Benjamin. 1969. *Black Abolitions*. New York. Oxford University Press, pp 40, 46, 47.

Redkey, Edwin S. 1969. Black Exodus. New Haven: Yale University Press. (An overview of Black Nationalist and Back-to-Africa Movements during this period).

Royal, Valentine. 1999. Quote from a conversation with Rev. Valentine Royal during the American Baptist Convention. Des Moines. June 21–25, 1999.

Simons, William J. 1887. *Men of Mark*. Cleveland, pp 136–140.

Tanner, Benjamin T. 1867. *Outlines of the History of the AME Church*. Baltimore, p 140.

Walker, Margaret. 1949. "We Have Been Believers" in Langston Hughes and Arna Bontemps, eds., *The Poetry of the Negro, 1746–1949*. New York: Doubleday and Company, Inc.

Ward, Samuel R. 1969. *Autobiography of a Fugitive Negro*. New York: Arno Press and *The New York Times*, p 64.

Washington, Joseph Jr. 1964. *Black Religion*. Boston: Beacon Press, pp 87–89, 292.

Work, John Wesley. 1915. *Folk Songs of the American Negro*. Nashville, pp 110–120.

Has Racial Diversity within Mainline Denominations in the United States Improved since the Civil Rights Movement of the 1960s?

Rev. Ernest L. Williams

Introduction

After the Civil Rights Movement of the 1960s, did the churches in the United States make any progress on the issue of race relations? Did the mainline churches in the United States make any forward movements for racial diversity within its congregations? Did the Civil Rights Movement fail? This study will examine the influence of the Civil Rights Movement on the churches in the United States relative to racial diversity. This study will further examine the current trend within the churches of the United States on the topic of racial diversity within the congregations. We will also examine two New Testament models to give insight into where we are now in terms of race relations within the mainline churches in the United States. Is there a correlation between how the churches in the United States deal with race and how the United States citizenry deals with race? This study will show that there has been progress made within our churches in this country on the issue of race relations that will prove that the Civil Rights Movement did have a positive impact on racial diversity of congregations in the United States.

Literature Review

Have the racial demographics of churches in the United States changed from the 1960s to 2018? In the 1960s, the White church in the United States struggled with race. Crouse points out that the Southern Baptist Convention (SBC), from the 1940s through the 1960s, had little influence on the 32,000 churches in the United States on the issue of racial injustices that had befallen African Americans. The Southern Baptist Convention made several attempts to encourage desegregation, but Crouse points out the Southern Baptist Convention was never the leading voice for Black equality.[1]

There was a dichotomy between the way White and Black clergy viewed the issue of race during the Civil Rights Movement. Evans states that the Rev. Billy Graham's preaching "for people to have a personal relationship with Jesus Christ" dominated evangelicals during the 1950s and '60s. Billy Graham and other evangelicals encouraged Dr. Martin Luther King and the leaders of the Civil Rights Movement to slow down and let things work themselves out through legislation. Graham even urged King to let God work out the racial issues in America.[2]

Dr. Martin Luther King, in his "Letter from a Birmingham Jail," responded to White clergy and rabbis who insisted that King was inciting violence and disobeying the law with protest marches and sit-ins. The White clergy charged King and the other civil rights leaders with not allowing God to change the situation. King, in his response, was surprised how the White clergy did not stand on the side of the Negro for racial and social justice.[3] The White church

[1] Stephen Gary Crouse, "A Missiological Evaluation of Southern Baptist Multiethnic Churches in the United States," (PhD diss., The Southern Baptist Theological Seminary, 2014), 116–118.

[2] Curtis urtis J. Evans, "White Evangelical Protestant Responses to the Civil Rights Movement," *Harvard Theological Review* 102 (2009): 253–254.

[3] James M. Washington, ed., *A Testament of Hope: The Essential Writings and Speeches of Martin Luther King, Jr.,* (San Francisco: Harper Collins Publishers, 1991), 299.

during and after the Civil Rights Movement of the 1960s proved ineffective at bridging the gap of racial division in America.

Despite the efforts of the Civil Rights Movement of the 1960s, most churches today remain racially segregated. Some of the mainline denominations (Catholics, Baptists, Methodist, Presbyterians, Church of Christ, Lutheran, Adventists, Pentecostals, and Episcopalians) have made several attempts to undo the wrongs of racial disharmony in the churches of the United States. For example, the SBC met in 1995 and adopted a "Resolution on Racial Reconciliation on the 150th Anniversary of the Southern Baptist Convention." Through the resolution, Southern Baptists renounced historic acts of racism, apologized to all African Americans for allowing and extending individual and systemic racism, and repented of these attitudes asking for forgiveness.[4]

Wright, Wallace, Wisnesky, Donnelly, Missari, and Zozula pointed out how the Presbyterian Church (USA), in its attempt to create multiethnic congregations has dedicated significant resources to that goal, including staff, grants, and internet resources. In the 1980s and 1990s, the Catholic Church in America changed its emphasis from cultural pluralism to multiculturalism.[5] For the most part, the mainline denominations have remained racially neutral in their congregational composition in the last fifty years. The only churches that seem to be connecting the theme of racial healing to congregational composition is the new multiethnic church. Multiethnic churches which have been started have done so with the purpose of bringing people of different races and ethnicities together.

---

4. Crouse, "A Missiological Evaluation," 138.
5. Bradley R. E. Wright et al., "Religion, Race, and Discrimination: A Field Experiment of How American Churches Welcome Newcomers," *JSSR* 54 (2015): 187.

How Racially Diverse Are U.S. Religious Groups?

% of each religious group in each racial/ethnic category, and each group's diversity score on the Herfindahl-Hirschman index

	White	Black	Asian	Mix/ Other	Latino	Index
Seventh-day Adventist	37%	32	8	8	15	9.1
Muslim	38	28	28	3	4	8.7
Jehovah's Witness	36	27	6		32	8.6
Buddhist	44	3	33	8	12	8.4
"Nothing in particular"	64	12	5	5	15	6.9
Catholic	59	3	3	2	34	6.7
All U.S. adults	66	12	4	4	15	6.6
Assemblies of God	66	3	5		25	6.2
Church of God (Cleveland, Tenn.)	65	3	3		28	6.2
Churches of Christ	69	16		4	10	6.1
American Baptist Churches USA	73	10		5	11	5.5
Atheist	78	3	7	2	10	4.7
Agnostic	79	3	4	4	9	4.5
Presbyterian Church in America	80	6	3	5	6	4.4
Orthodox Christian	81	8	3	2	6	4.2
Anglican Church	83			12	4	3.7
Church of God in Christ	5	84		4	8	3.5
Southern Baptist Convention	85	6		5	3	3.4
Mormon	85			5	8	3.4
Presbyterian Church (U.S.A.)	88	5		3	4	2.8
Church of the Nazarene	88		2	3	7	2.7
Unitarian	88			7	4	2.7
United Church of Christ	89			8	2	2.5
Jewish	90	2	2	2	4	2.3
Episcopal Church	90		4	3	2	2.3
Hindu	4	2	91		2	2.1
United Methodist Church	94			2	2	1.4
African Methodist Episcopal Church	2	94			3	1.4
Lutheran Church-Missouri Synod	95			2	2	1.2
Evang. Lutheran Church in America	96				2	1.0
National Baptist Convention		99				0.2

MORE DIVERSE ▲ ▼ LESS DIVERSE

Source: 2014 Religious Landscape Study.
Note: Figures may not add to 100% due to rounding. Blacks, whites, Asians and others/mixed include only those who are not Latino. Latinos include people of all races.

PEW RESEARCH CENTER

Some researchers see the change toward racially diverse churches as positive for both Black and White Christians. Cobb, Perry, and Dougherty conducted a study of 1,485 churchgoers across ethnic and racial differences. Of those surveyed, 21 percent attended multiracial congregations.[6] Kathleen Garces-Foley defines multiracial congregation on a 20/80 ratio, where no racial group makes up more than 80 percent of the congregation.[7]

The graphic (Figure 1)[8] by the Pew Research Center illustrates the denominations that are ranked from racially less to racially more diverse. For the most part, the figure shows that there has not been a drastic change in the racial composition of churches in the United States since the 1960s. Richard Pitt agrees with researcher Gerardo Marti that churches can play an integral role in undoing the United States racial divide.[9] However, Marti believes "achieving true religious integration between blacks and whites seems nearly impossible in the face of racial obstacles."[10]

In considering the issue of racial diversity within the churches in the United States, research shows that this nation has always struggled with race. The Civil Rights Movement made the White churches aware of the sin of racism, but neither the White church, nor the Black church proved capable of amending the disparities of racial diversity within the mainline denominations in the United States. From the 1990s to the present, multiracial congregations have been on the rise. From the research, we cannot conclude that the Civil Rights Movement was the catalyst to this emergence of the multiethnic church. If there has been any growth with respect to racial

---

6. Ryon J. Cobb, Samuel L. Perry, and Kevin D. Dougherty, "United by Faith? Race/Ethnicity, Congregational Diversity, and Explanations of Racial Inequality," *Sociology of Religion* 76 (2015): 185.

7. Kathleen Garces-Foley, "Multiethnic Congregations," 63.

8. Michael Lipka, "The Most and Least Racially Diverse U.S. Religious Groups," Pew Research Center, http://www.pewresearch.org/fact-tank/2015/07/27/the-most-and-least-racially-diverse-u-s-religious-groups/.

9. Richard Pitt, "Fear of a Black Pulpit? Real Racial Transcendence Versus Cultural Assimilation in Multiracial Churches," *JSSR* 49 (2010): 222.

10. Gerard Marti, "The Religious Integration of African Americans into Diverse Churches," *JSSR* 49 (2010): 201.

diversity within the churches of the United States, God would be the agent of change.

Data Collection

This collection of data consists of findings from interviews conducted by the author with people of diverse backgrounds who attend various churches in North Alabama and in Tennessee and who were aware of racial tension in the 1960s. Secondly, we explore the New Testament for hidden truths about race and worship. Six people were interviewed and were asked three questions. The first question, "What was your view of the integration of churches in the 1960s? (Did you believe that black and white people could worship together in the 1960s?)" The second question, "Has your view changed since that time?" The third question, "In what way did the Civil Rights Movement of the 1960s have an impact on the white and black churches in the Southeastern United States? (Did the Civil Rights Movement in anyway influence your view of the integration of churches?)"

The responses are as follows. Leslie believes that the way things were, Blacks and Whites could not worship together in the 1960s. She said that Blacks should stay in their churches, and Whites should stay in theirs. Since then, Leslie believed that some change has occurred, and she is optimistic.[11] Carter 1 and Carter 2 believed then and still believe that there should be no reason why Blacks and Whites cannot worship together. The Civil Rights Movement did not influence their awareness of racial harmony. Their conviction about people has always been about pleasing God. Carter 1 said, "I have never had any trouble with black people." Carter 2 said, "God said to get along with everybody and to not treat people different."[12]

[11.] Mary Leslie, (Member of the Mount Zion Missionary Baptist Church, Toney, Alabama, born March 25, 1919, African American), in discussion with the author, March 2018.

[12.] Homer "Buddy" and Betty Carter, (Members of the Cash Point Baptist Church, Ardmore, TN, Mr. Carter, born, April 6, 1922, Mrs. Carter, born, January 21,

Beverly, who was a childhood member of the Dexter Avenue Baptist Church, was baptized by Dr. Martin Luther King, Jr. He said of the 1960s and Whites and Blacks worshipping together that "I did not give it much thought then." Beverly participated in the marches in Montgomery and Selma. Beverly witnessed Black and White people holding hands singing "We Shall Over Overcome." Beverly's views today: "In an ideal world, people of all ethnicities should worship together. However, in the real world, that dream is difficult to achieve." In terms of the impact of the Civil Rights Movement and the diversity of churches, Beverly believes, "I don't think the movement perpetuated the coming together of blacks and whites to worship together. Nevertheless, the movement did light a fuse on the divide of black and white churches. The divide is real." Beverly said that in terms of Blacks and Whites who came together in the 1960s, "People came together to confront a common enemy called racism."[13]

Hobbs remembered White people who attended their all-Black church in the late fifties and early sixties. She was always in favor of all people worshipping together. Hobbs believed that the Civil Rights Movement did have a positive impact on the way Black and White people viewed God and each other.[14] Monroe said, "Many churches today are integrated. There are more blacks in white churches than whites in black churches." Monroe went on to say, "Church integration is voluntary whereas school integration was mandatory." Monroe's views have changed since the Civil Rights Movement. Monroe concluded, "Race relations have improved because open violence on integration is not acceptable and prohibited by law."[15]

1943, Caucasians), in discussion with the author, March 2018. [Since that time Mr. Carter has passed from this life into eternal rest.]

13. Creigs Beverly, PhD. (Retired Professor of Social Work, Wayne State University, Fulbright Scholar, born September 9, 1942) in discussion with the author, March 2018.

14. Martha Hobbs (Member of the Mount Zion Baptist Church, Toney, Alabama, born October 13, 1924, African America), in discussion with author, March 2018.

15. Donald Monroe (Retired history and special education teacher, Huntsville, Alabama, attended Oakwood College, 1964–1968, Participated in the

Interestingly, the Bible is a valuable resource in the study of racial diversity. How does the Bible deal with the question of racial diversity within the New Testament church? According to Acts 2, the church had its beginnings with believers from various races ranging from Palestine, Asia, Europe, the Middle East, and Africa.[16] The first-century church was not exempt from racial disharmony. Acts 6 opens with racial conflict within the church. When the Grecian Christians complained against the Jewish Christians concerning their widows being neglected in the daily distribution of commodities, the church leaders immediately dealt with the problem. They were able to deal with the matter efficiently and successfully through direct dialogue.[17]

The last biblical reference in this study is Acts 6:9. This verse highlights a Jewish synagogue composed of freed slaves from Africa and Asia Minor. This Jewish synagogue was composed of people who were once slaves. Even in the first century, people of faith found it more acceptable to worship with people of similar lifestyles, background, and ancestry.

Results Summary

The data in this report is consistent with the view of Scripture that people of different ethnic backgrounds have always struggled with racial diversity coupled with the worship of God. Today, some people seem optimistic about the future. Realistically, people seem to feel comfortable worshipping with other people with similar backgrounds and experiences as their own. Included in this summary is a quote on the subject from Pastor Robert Morris. Pastor Morris is a White pastor of a 31,000-multiethnic-member congregation on six campuses in the greater Dallas/Fort Worth area. "The answer to racism lies primarily in the church, not the government...and now

---

Montgomery and Selma Marches during the 1960s, born October 15, 1938), in discussion with the author, March 2018.

[16.] Acts 2:7–11

[17.] Acts 6:1–6

that white pastors are waking up to the pain that black people have felt, it is in many ways a hopeful time."[18]

Conclusion and Recommendations

In evaluating the data, three conclusive statements are inferred. One, White and Black churches have made little progress in terms of racially diverse congregations among mainline denominations. Secondly, the data does not indicate whether the success of the Civil Rights Movement affected change in the racial composition of mainline denominations in the United States. Thirdly, the data does show that the mainline churches have not made dramatic changes in their racial composition but that a new movement has emerged in the form of the multiethnic church. It is undetermined in this study if the multiethnic congregation is a byproduct of the Civil Rights Movement. Further study will be needed to investigate the positive and negative attributes of the multiethnic congregation with respect to race. This current study sought to focus on what impact did the Civil Rights Movement have on mainline denominations in the United States.

The six people interviewed were eyewitnesses to the 1960s Civil Rights Movement; they all had one common theme: even though they had different opinions about the past, they were all optimistic about the future. They believed that if race relations were to improve in the churches in the United States, God would have to bring about the change. Concerning the Scriptures, the Bible recognized the diversity of race as acceptable to the first-century church and Jewish synagogues. Future studies are needed to give a thorough report of biblical references to this subject of racial diversity within the churches in the New Testament.

In seeking to understand race in the United States of America, the church becomes the testing ground for racial harmony. The

---

18. Campbell, Robertson, "A Quiet Exodus: Why Black Worshipers Are Leaving White Evangelical Churches," *The New York Times*, March 9, 2018, https://www.nytimes.com/2018/03/09/us/blacks-evangelical-churches.html.

author submits that even though there has been progress with respect to race in the churches in the United States, this country still has a way to go. Being optimistic about the future, we trust God to help us achieve this goal of racial harmony within the churches of America.

BIBLIOGRAPHY

Cobb, Ryon J., Samuel L. Perry, and Kevin D. Dougherty. "United by Faith? Race/Ethnicity, Congregational Diversity, and Explanations of Racial Inequality." *Sociology of Religion* 76 (2015): 179–180.

Crouse, Stephen G. "A Missiological Evaluation of Southern Baptist Multiethnic Churches in The United States." PhD diss., The Southern Baptist Theological Seminary, 2014.

Evans, Curtis J. "White Evangelical Protestant Responses to the Civil Rights Movement." *HTR* 102 (2009): 245–273.

Garces-Foley, Kathleen. "Multiethnic Congregations." The Christian Reflection Project/Baylor University. https://www.baylor. edu/content/services/document.php/110977.pdf.

"Homogeneity." Oxford Dictionaries. https://en.oxforddictionaries. com/definition/homogeneity.

Lipka, Michael. "The Most and Least Racially Diverse U.S. Religious Groups." Pew Research Center. 27 July 2015. http://www.pewresearch.org/fact-tank/2015/07/27/ the-most-and-least-racially-diverse-u-s-religious-groups/.

Marti, Gerardo. "Affinity, Identity, and Transcendence: The Experience of Religious Racial Integration in Multiracial Churches." *JSSR* 48 (2009): 53–68.

Marti, Gerardo. "The Religious Integration of African Americans into Diverse Churches." *JSSR* 49 (2010): 201.

Pitt, Richard. "Fear of a Black Pulpit? Real Racial Transcendence Versus Cultural Assimilation in Multiracial Churches." *JSSR* 49 (2010): 218–223.

Robertson, Campbell. "A Quiet Exodus: Why Black Worshipers Are Leaving White Evangelical Churches." *The New York Times.*

March 9, 2018, https://www.nytimes.com/2018/03/09/us/
blacks-evangelical-churches.html.

Wright, Bradley, Michael Wallace, Annie Scola Wisnesky, Christopher
M. Donnelly, Stacy Missari, and Christine Zozula. "Religion,
Race, and Discrimination: A Field Experiment of How
American Churches Welcome Newcomers." *JSSR* 54 (2015):
185–204.

Washington, James M., ed. *A Testament of Hope: The Essential
Writings and Speeches of Martin Luther King, Jr.* San Francisco:
HarperCollins, 1991.

IN THE BELLY OF THE WHALE: CULTURAL DIMENSIONS OF AFRICAN AMERICAN INCARCERATION AND REHABILITATION

Creigs C. Beverly, PhD, and Robert E. Burns, STD

Our approach to the problems of the church's response to the incarceration of African American men involves four central contentions. First, American culture, defined by and controlled primarily in the interest of White males of European descent, has never functioned fully to enfranchise African Americans. Thus, an approach to the problem in terms of its cultural dimensions from "inside the belly of the whale" is appropriate. Second, social deviance resulting in the incarceration of African Americans is understood as a form of compensatory behavior often designed to compensate for personal impotence in a culture that perceives and responds to Black men as if they were nonpersons. Third, the rehabilitation of African Americans, once they have been incarcerated, is a cruel paradox of the highest order. The question has to be raised: rehabilitation from what to what? To state the matter differently, what are the consequences of placing a healthy fish in a polluted pond? Unless the pond is made healthy, it will, in all probability, reinfect the healthy fish. Finally, incarceration and rehabilitation should both be viewed as reactionary responses to a people whose social reality demands proactive and radical intervention, if the "ought" is ever to render the "is" null and void.

In the Belly of the Whale

Depending on the source, culture takes on many different yet related definitions. For purposes of this essay, culture is operationally defined as the cumulative experiences of a people, indexed by time. These experiences converge to provide a profile of what was, what is, and what can reasonably be expected. As eloquently expressed by C. Eric Lincoln, human society is dynamic; it is never a static accomplishment capable of complete realization in a lifetime or a generation. Rather, it is always in process—always becoming what it is, always different from what it was, yet never what it will be (Lincoln 1971).

It has always been the fervent hope of African Americans that there will someday be a nexus between words and deeds and that a resulting synthesis will create a new American thesis that no longer consigns them to the role of antithesis. This day has yet to come and, as a consequence, the proportionate share of goods and services, paid for in over four hundred years of blood, sweat, and tears, remains elusive; more myth than reality.

Thus, the symbolism of being in "the belly of the whale" takes on meaning. The whale represents American culture and society, a society that African Americans helped to build, to grow, to become wealthy, and to extend its influence worldwide, even into the far reaches of space. While oppressed and suppressed in the belly of the whale, African Americans, in spite of the whale's destructive digestive juices, provided the nation with a range of servants, from cotton pickers to neurosurgeons; they produced the food which has made the whale obese, while the food producers became increasingly frail.

In a speech to the national convention of the National Association for the Advancement of Colored People, held in Detroit in July 1989, Dr. Louis Sullivan, secretary of the US Department of Health and Human Services, reeled off an alarming set of statistics. The average life expectancy for African Americans declined two years in a row, from 1984 to 1986. It was 69.7 years in 1984; 69.5 in 1985; and 69.4 in 1986. The mortality rate for African American infants is twice that of White infants.

Homicide is the second leading cause of death among all African American young people between the ages of fifteen to twenty-four. Illegal drug use has reached epidemic proportions, compounded by the AIDS epidemic (Sullivan 1989). One needs to add to these statistics that today, African American men are 6 percent of the US population but 46 percent of all prisoners; that more African American men are in prison than are currently enrolled in colleges; that the most rapidly growing group of poor and homeless persons is single women with children, many of whom are African Americans; that there are unacceptably high levels of teenage pregnancy and school dropout among African American youth throughout the nation.

Through it all, African Americans, rooted in a spirit of collective self-confidence, have resisted every sign and symbol of enthrallment and have refused accommodation to a system that consistently seeks to impeach their humanity (Lincoln 1971). Leonard E. Barrett calls this will to live, to survive, and thrive—Soul Force (Barrett 1974).

"Soul Force" in Black talk describes that quality of life that has enabled Black people to survive the horrors of their "diaspora." The experience of slavery, and its later repercussions, still remain to be dealt with, and "Soul" signifies the moral and emotional fiber of the Black man that enables him to see his dilemma clearly and at the same time encourages and sustains him in his struggles. "Force" connotes strength, power, intense effort, and a will to live. The combined words "Soul Force" describe the racial inheritance of the New World African; it is that which characterizes his lifestyle, his worldview, and his endurance under conflict. It is his frame of reference vis-à-vis the wider world and his blueprint for the struggle from bondage to freedom. Soul Force is that power of the Black man which turns sorrow into joy, crying into laughter, and defeat into victory. It is patience while suffering, determination while frustrated, and hope while in despair. It derives its impetus from the ancestral heritage of Africa, its refinement from the bondage of slavery, and its continuing vitality from the conflict of the present. It expresses itself collectively as well as through charismatic leaders. In addition, it can express itself in states of acquiescence, avoidance, and separation. So there is no end to the permutations and combinations of the restless "soul." Soul is visceral rather than intellectual, irrational rather than rational, it is art rather than logic (Barrett 1974).

Nonetheless, no one can ignore the devastating consequences of life in a nation which continues to debate whether a select few will be free or whether all persons who reside within its territory will be free. Much of the violence and crime in this society can be accounted for because people (disproportionately African Americans) are denied access to the fullness of what it means to be human.

Compensatory Behaviors

Why does anyone engage in compensatory behavior? Compensation, in the lexicon of psychology, refers to psychological mechanisms by which feelings of inferiority, frustration, or failure in one of several arenas of life are counterbalanced by achievement in others. This point is clearly evident in the following example.

In a recent conversation with two young African American drug dealers in a major urban colony of the United States, each was asked whether anything, short of death or incarceration, could deter them from continuing to sell drugs. The response of the first young man (translated) sounded like this: "It is much too late for me. Someone should have gotten to me a long time ago. I know what my chances of being killed are, and I know what my chances are of going to jail for life, but until then, I have it all." The second young man (translated) said, "American society sets forth a profile of what it means to be a *normal* contributing member of society. Then the same society, through neglect, indifference, and inadequate supports, makes sure many people can't achieve that profile, especially Black men. Then the same society comes right back and blames you for being abnormal. Well, I want to tell you that I am very normal, given my circumstances and my reality. If you want me to stop selling drugs, then provide me with a viable alternative. If you aren't prepared to do this, then I have nothing else to say, and I will not stop selling drugs, as my brother just said, until I am dead or in jail."

What you have in these two examples are young Black men compensating in a society that they feel has dealt them less than an equal amount of chips. These are examples of what Erich Fromm calls "people to whom life has denied the capacity for any positive expression of their specifically human powers" (Fromm 1971).

It should be made explicitly clear that these examples of compensatory behavior are not intended to justify antisocial lifestyles, particularly when such lifestyles (as in the case of selling drugs in African American communities) wreak personal, family, social, and communal destruction. The important point here is that without some coherent explanation of behavior, it becomes virtually impossible to fashion a rational strategy for corrective intervention.

It is important to ask why knowledge to prevent social deviance is not more effectively utilized in a society where behavior has been subjected to years of empirical research. For example, it has been known for many years that children who have excellent pre-school educational experiences do much better in later schooling, have fewer behavioral and adjustment problems, and tend to be more successful in life than children who did not have the same advantage. Yet society is still reluctant to invest $3,000 on the front end of life to ensure the best possible outcome for youth but seems willing to invest $25,000 a year to keep them in prison. One can only conclude that the manufacture of deviance, particularly in the case of certain population cohorts, such as African Americans, if not a conspiracy, is at least an example of human neglect which can be characterized as criminal.

Ralph Ellison expressed this concern in a famous quotation:

> I am invisible because you refuse to see me. You
> often wonder if you really exist in the real world.
> You ache with the pain to convince yourself that
> you do exist in the real world—that you are part
> of all of the sound and all of the anguish—and
> you strike out with your fists and you curse and
> you swear to make them recognize you—but
> alas, it is seldom successful. To whom can I be

accountable and why should I be, when you refuse to see me. (Ellison 1952)

Rehabilitation

In a classical sense, rehabilitation refers to the attempt to restore someone to a condition of health or useful and constructive activity—to restore to a former state. In this paper, rehabilitation is focused on African Americans who have been incarcerated and the problem of their subsequent restoration to law-abiding, constructive, and productive human beings. As we stated at the outset, the question has to be posed. Rehabilitation from what, to what? This is a crucial question when it pertains to those African Americans whose social realities prior to incarceration were such that *options* for law-abiding, constructive, and productive lives were marginal to nonexistent.

The rehabilitation of prisoners, irrespective of race, is most difficult because the stigma of being an *ex-convict* is an awesome burden to carry. But when one is both an ex-convict and an African American, overcoming the effects of this dual burden is at times almost impossible. To put this into perspective, the Reverend Charles Adams, cited by *Ebony Magazine* as one of the ten most prominent preachers in America, shared that:

> In all of my travels around the country and the world, I am more and more convinced that Black people are the most despised and hated people on Earth.

These words were spoken in the context of the need for African Americans to reaffirm and reanchor themselves in the Black church in order to acquire the strength to continue fighting systemic injustices and human underdevelopment. It was a call to return to what Barrett called Soul Force—that power of the Black man which turns sorrow into joy, crying into laughter, and defeat into victory (Barrett

1974)—the power of patience while suffering, determination while frustrated, and hope in the midst of despair.

All of this means that any attempt to focus the rehabilitation of African American prisoners solely on individual transformation, disconnected from the quality of life in African American communities, is a cruel hoax. It is a cruel hoax because the two are inseparable. In most circumstances, it is impossible to have a healthy individual without a healthy community. If a person's community does not provide opportunities for decent, safe, affordable, and sanitary housing, gainful and meaningful employment, high quality and functional education, access to medical care and security from the ravishes of crime and drugs, to what then do you return the "rehabilitated" prisoner? How many times have we heard repeated offenders say, "I had no other options"?

This leads to the summary thesis of this paper which is that incarceration and subsequent rehabilitation are reactionary responses to people already consigned to the status of being disposable in a society which repeatedly demonstrates its disdain for them. If there is any doubt about this, note the comment of President George Bush's budget director, Richard Darman: "If forced to make a choice, I prefer to spend money on the space station rather than housing the homeless" (Kupcinet 1989). All of us are aware that the problem of homelessness among African American is most severe, not to mention the horrific state of disrepair of many houses in what we may call the urban colonies of the United States.

The African American Church and Progressive Action

In order to move away from reactionary responses to incarceration and the rehabilitation of African Americans, progressive and developmental approaches are required. Since the African American church is one of only a few institutions in African American communities that are able to act autonomously, it can serve as a centerpiece for addressing conditions of life which force many people to adopt forms of behavior which result in incarceration. To do this requires that the church set forth an agenda based upon holistic social development goals and implement these in all communities.

We begin with the assumption that social development occurs best in communities that hold human values paramount and view the maintenance of life and improvement of the quality of life as ultimate goals. Further, when African American people are regarded as subjects of the world, capable of acting upon the world and, in the process, contributing to the betterment of humankind, the following social development goals are essential (Beverly 1984):

1. The eradication of social and economic injustice owing to discrimination based on ideology, religion, race, sex, class, and ethnicity.
2. The elimination of hunger, disease, and violence, since these are absolute threats to physical survival, and the introduction of prevention as the cornerstone of action versus reaction after the fact.
3. The creation of participatory mechanisms (a political system) which ensures that every person has an equal opportunity to influence the decisions which affect his/her life.
4. The adoption of a policy of relative self-reliance which makes maximum use of resources, both human and material, endemic to a country, and which balances technology transfer and importation according to developmental stages.
5. The commitment to the elimination of any and all violations of human rights to ensure that no one loses the opportunity to pursue life in a manner calculated to promote personal dignity.
6. The removal of illiteracy from the social fabric of the community and the organization, operation, and maintenance of educational systems which develop the fullest potential of every community member within his/her capabilities, so that education no longer serves the role of social stratification but, instead, of social unification.

7. The construction of decent, safe, and sanitary housing for all.

8. The creation of the necessary infrastructures of water, sewage systems, roads, communications, transportation, etc.—supportive of maximum human capacity.

9. A view of the family as the crucible in which personal and community well-being is developed and should be accorded the respect and support necessary for the effective implementation of its crucial responsibilities.

10. The development of policies which keep population growth in balance with the community's capacity to meet the needs of its members.

11. A respect for the non-material needs of community members as these are reflected in religious preferences, forms, and practices.

The African American church must accept these challenges and join with the hopeful element in all histories of the human struggle for community. The church must help us reclaim once again the great hidden capacities of African Americans to dream, to imagine a new American society, and to become full participants in its re-creation. Only then will we be enabled, with courage and hope, to burst the barriers of all the political, economic, and social structures of oppression that now hold us in bondage to our worst selves (Harding 1981).

The following "Theological Declaration on the Prison System" was written by twelve imprisoned students in the New York Theological Seminary program at Sing Sing Correctional Facility, Ossining, New York.

A Theological Declaration on the Prison System

1. We are twelve imprisoned students in the New York Theological Seminary program at Sing Sing Correctional Facility, Ossining, New York.
2. We have committed ourselves to theological reflection in order to discover God's presence within our prison experience and to seek God's guidance in confronting the oppressive elements within that experience.
3. We have reflected on the harmful and contradictory effects of long-term imprisonment on both prisoners and on society.
    *   Prisons destroy the sense of selfhood through endless regimentation.
    *   Prisons destroy self-confidence and initiative through the constant state of dependency.
    *   Prisons destroy "rootedness" founded in the family or any other healthy relationship through prolonged confinement in an archaic unnatural environment.
    *   Prisons destroy the willingness of human beings to trust other human beings and destroys the capacity to enter into loving and sharing relationships.
    *   Prisons destroy and prevent spiritual growth.
4. Continuously victimized by false dilemmas and reactionary violence systematically entrenched, prisoners confront:
    *   direct, massive force
    *   symbolic, repressive violence; for example, the "club carrying" of prison officials
    *   Modified brainwashing, the objective of which is to destroy positive values and social contacts
    *   Psychological death (a well-known practice in prisons that involves the use of medical science as a means of control through sterilization, Thorazine, and other drugs)

5. We prisoners have come to understand that "the devil will put you to the test by having some of you thrown into prison" (Rev. 2:10).

6. But God is justice (Job 37:23), and an unjust system will cause the oppressed to rise up against it (Amos 6). As prisoners, we ask that judgement run down as waters, and righteousness as a mighty stream (Amos 5:24). For human beings truly perish in this "valley of dry bones" (Ezekiel 37:1, 2).

7. We hear the good news proclaimed by Jesus in the synagogue at Nazareth:

He has sent me to proclaim liberty to the captives...to set free the oppressed, and to announce that the time has come when the Lord will save his people. (Luke 4:18–19, *Good News Bible*)

8. We believe that God's will can be done within prison walls, and that it is the moral responsibility of administration, officers, civilian faculty, and prisoners to work together in all areas that will fulfill the needs of the majority of the people within the prison system.

9. We understand the cries of society for the curtailment of crime and for protection against those who violate society's laws. But we believe that prison should be a place for holistic restoration and reform rather than solely for punishment.

10. As students in the New York Theological Seminary program, we believe that the prisons could benefit from our contribution to programs that could take advantage of our skills. As incarcerated theologians and intellectuals, we believe that we have special responsibility and leadership roles in prison ministry and in the prison community.

11. We call on the churches to assume direct responsibility for church matters within the prison, effectively removing the affairs of the prison church from corrections and/or civil

authorities. Church-monitored community review boards could ensure that the prison ministry serves the spiritual needs of the incarcerated.

12. We call for support, expansion, and constant evaluation of all prison educational and vocational programs. These programs should conform to standards established by the Board of Cooperative Educational Services BOCES, and other community and private sector programs.

13. We call for the improvement of prison counseling, with more and better qualified counselors, smaller caseloads, and increased contacts.

14. We call for the establishment and upgrading of pre-release programs that incorporate the contributions of community representatives, business/employment agencies, the churches, and the parole board. Presently, pre-release programs utilize community resources, however, there is little accountability for the effective use of these resources. Community-based agencies funded with LEAA (Law Enforcement Assistance Association) funds should be required to procure actual jobs rather than simply letters of reasonable assurance.

15. We call for an extension of the Family Reunion Program to those with common-law marriages, especially when there are children involved. "Family" should be determined by non-support law accountability or surrogate parent status attained by serving as household head prior to incarceration. (Non-support law accountability means that a prisoner must support a child born out of wedlock by law. The same prisoner is however denied family reunion privileges with that common-law family inside the correctional institution).

16. We call for the provision of appropriate service to prisoners for both pre-existing mental illness and prison-incurred emotional disturbance. There is need to upgrade psychological treatment.

17. We call on the churches to implement a program whereby a committee of concerned Christians would monitor and ensure that visitors to correctional facilities are not subjected to unreasonable dress codes. (Female visitors are frequently required to change a blouse or skirt in order to conform to arbitrary judgments about the modesty of their clothing.)

18. We call for a reevaluation of the classification system; all meaningful adjustments through education, vocational, or therapeutic programs should be taken into consideration in the modification of classifications.

19. We call for a neutral agency to review all cases of cruelty, brutality, and insensitivity within the prison system.

20. We invite responses to our Theological Declaration from prison officials, church people, other prisoners, and all concerned citizens. Responses may be sent to Rev. J. Karel Boersma, The Reformed Church of Beacon, Ferry Street at Academy, Beacon, N.Y. 12508.

21. We, the undersigned, commit ourselves to the implementation of this Theological Declaration and to a new beginning for God's will within the prison system. (The following signatures are appended.)

George Franklin, Charles Frazier, Morris Howard, Donald Jones, Angel Rosado Maldonado, Julio Cesar Maldonado, Roy Melvin, Herbert Payne, Robert Dawad Smith, Robert Turner, Leon O. Woods, and Henry Johnson.

REFERENCES

Barrett, Leonard E. 1974. *Soul-Force: African Heritage in Afro-American Religion*. New York: Anchor Press/ Doubleday, pp 1–2.

Beverly, Creigs. 1984. "Social Development and National Development: The African Context," Research Monograph as part of Fulbright Professorship, University of Ghana.

Ellison, Ralph. 1952. *Invisible Man*. New York: Vintage Books.

Fromm, Erich. 1971. *The Heart of Man: It's Genius for Good and Evil*. New York: Harper and Row, pp. 26–27.

Harding, Vincent. 1981. *There Is a River*. New York: Harcourt Brace Jovanovich., p. xxv.

Kupcinet, Irv. July 1989. *Chicago Sun-Times*.

Lincoln, C. Eric. Summer 1971. "The Negro College and Cultural Change." *Daedalus*, p. 605.

Sullivan, Louis. July 1989. "Health Status of Blacks in America." NAACP Convention Speech, Detroit, Michigan.

Questions for Study
and Discussion

1. In their contribution to the discussion, Creigs C. Beverly and Robert Burns claim that four factors negatively condition the church's response to the incarceration of African American men. Discuss and evaluate these factors.

2. Do you agree that the symbolism of being in "the belly of the whale" accurately reflects the situation in which we find ourselves in American society? What do you understand by the authors' concept of "Soul Force"? Are you satisfied with these metaphors? How does having "Soul Force" qualify the experience of being "in the belly of the whale"? Since they are concerned about "cultural dimensions," what should be the cultural emphasis of any program of prisoner rehabilitation that takes seriously what Beverly and Burns are saying about Black oppression and survival?

3. What do the authors suggest must be the *cultural* responsibility of African American prison ministries as opposed to a narrow focus on *individual transformation*?

4. Discuss the eleven developmental goals of "progressive action" that the authors recommend for the African American community. Obviously, these are intended as preventative measures to stem the tide of Black male incarceration. Which ones seem possible for incorporation in the program of a local congregation trying to change the neighborhood in which it is located? Which ones would the group eliminate as too difficult or unrealistic?

5. "The Theological Declaration on the Prison System" is a remarkable document written in 1988 by men at Sing Sing who were students in the New York Theological Seminary Master of Professional Studies Program. Discuss the points it makes and evaluate their importance for a church-sponsored program of prison reform and/or abolition.
6. How can this challenge be communicated to the churches?

MODEL FOR PREVENTION AND SUPPORT: TRANSPOSITION FROM JAIL CELL TO CHURCH PEW

Dr. Creigs Beverly

Every human experience rests upon some previous experience, and every possibility for tomorrow is contingent to some other possibility which was realized yesterday. Human possibility is created at the intersection of time, place, and circumstance. Manipulate any one of these variables and the life chances of any given individual will be changed. If all the world is a stage, as Shakespeare alleged it to be, then history is the backdrop for the play, and the parts we play and the possibilities inherent in them are at least in part conditioned by other actors, who at other times have stood before the same footlights. Like us, they played their roles in terms of their possibilities.

—C. Eric Lincoln

This is a model for prevention and support in relation to interrupting the current freeway which leads to prison that far too many African American men and women are traveling upon. Within the social and behavioral sciences, there are two major or primary prevention models. They are person-centered prevention and systems-centered prevention.

In order to address effectively a model for prevention and support designed to remove African American men and women from this freeway, it is necessary to discuss and interface both models. The essential thesis of this paper is that person-centered prevention and systems-centered prevention are inseparable, bound together through organic reciprocity and mutual interdependence.

Person-centered prevention

Person-centered prevention is defined as activities designed to develop, maintain, and enhance knowledge, values, and skills that lower the vulnerability index of individuals. To state this differently, this model seeks to strengthen the internal capacity of individuals to navigate, negotiate, and orchestrate their social realities in ways and means consistent with maximization of human potential. These abilities or capabilities are important for all human beings to master, but they are especially important for African American males—given their current status in America.

Dr. Lawrence Gary, distinguished professor of social work at Virginia Commonwealth University and former director of the Institute for Urban Research at Howard University, has done some groundbreaking research on the attributes of successful Black men in America. Dr. Gary has identified ten such attributes which should form the core of any effort to strengthen the internal capacities of Black men to survive and thrive in this culture. These attributes are as follows:

- **Early direction in life**. Black men need to develop early life goal plans as a means to focus their energies and as a barometer against which they can make and measure decisions.
- **Early discipline**. Black men need someone to keep them in check, to pull their coattails when they are getting off track, to put some parameters on their behavior.
- **Early focus on literacy**. Black men need to be encouraged to master their worlds through education—reading, writ-

ing, computation, and general social, economic, and political literacy.

- **Early focus on culture**. Black men need to study, understand, and appreciate Black culture. The format here is triangular, what was, what is not and what is possible.

- **Early religious orientation**. Black men need to be grounded in the Black Church. They need to have their physical selves centered in a spiritual base.

- **Early respect for Black women**. Black men must be taught to respect all Black women and to understand that when God created Eve, God did not take the bone from Adam's foot (so Black women were not created to be kicked around by Black men); nor did God take the bone from Adam's hand (so Black women were not created to be slapped around by Black men); rather God took the bone from the side of Adam, which means that Black women were created to stand as equals with Black men.

- **Early work ethic**. Black men need to be exposed to work early and develop an appreciation and respect for all work. This is also a part of discipline, time management, accountability, reliability, and economic responsibility.

- **Early opportunities for public speaking**. Skills in public speaking build confidence, sharpen one's verbal skills, and lessen the need to use physical force.

- **Early commitment to family life and responsibility**. Black men need to discover early the meaning of fatherhood, provider, protector, supporter, teacher, counselor, and friend, and to see the family as the core of all human civility and human development.

- **Being an early asset to, rather than a burden of the Black community**. Black men need to develop an early sense of community (common- unity) and learn how to develop, sustain, and enhance the community.

Other scholars and observers of the African American condition may expand upon or modify these attributes, but few, if any, disagree with them. As a consequence, within the last few years, a major movement has occurred in Black communities under the designation of "Rites of Passage" where these and other exercises are now being made available to young Black men. This movement is well within the category of person-centered prevention. In the Appendix, Tables 1, 2, 3, and 4 provide four modules which can give direction to churches wishing to initiate such a program.

Systems-centered prevention

The second model under review here is systems-centered prevention, which is designed to ensure that the major institutions that impact the quality of Black male life operate to promote and enhance the quality of their life. For example, many school districts are experimenting with establishing all-male academies or all-male classes within gender-integrated schools. Many churches are now running weekend academies for Black males.

Fundamentally important to systems-centered prevention in the African American community is the perspective from which institutional structures and arrangements are viewed. This perspective is important because it determines the focus of institutional change initiatives. For example, European culture is preoccupied with the disease model and spends considerable energy identifying pathology—or what is wrong. The end result is too often "blaming the victim," e.g., placing causation for pathology at the individual level with little attention given to the relationship between personal pathology and institutional pathology.

The key here is that the health of the individual is inseparable from the institutions with which he/she interfaces on a regular basis.

Examples of the effects of this shortsightedness are replete. If millions of African American people, due to economic discrimination, are without access to high quality health care, can you then place blame for health difficulties at the personal level? If public schools are doing an inadequate job of educating youth, can you blame the youth for being miseducated, undereducated, or not educated at all? If Black men are sent to prison for crimes disproportionate to other ethnic and racial groups that commit the same crimes, can you then blame Black men for being in prison in numbers disproportionate to their percentage of the population? The answer is certainly not!

It is important to acknowledge that the foregoing analogy does not remove personal responsibility and personal accountability for one's choices, but it is to support the notion that there is a reciprocal relationship between the person and his/her environment. As expressed in the epigraph by C. Eric Lincoln, human possibility is a function of the interplay between time, place, and circumstance. Because of the particular history of African Americans in this culture, time, place, and circumstance, they have not usually been the most positive or conducive factors for maintaining human potential.

A sociobiological perspective

The perspective deemed most appropriate for viewing institutional effects on African Americans is sociobiological rather than psychosocial. The sociobiological perspective views human behavior as it is influenced from the social to the personal rather than from the personal to the social. The psychosocial model assumes that corrections in a person's thinking processes, attitudes, and decisions can alter the external (social) reality. The sociobiological perspective further undergirds the notion that changes in an oppressive social reality can lead to changes in how a person responds to that reality.

Perhaps one of the clearest illustrations of the differential outcomes associated with the particular perspective one chooses to use in examining reality is that provided by Dr. Louis King of the Fanon Center of the Drew Medical School at UCLA. Dr. King understands the deficit perspective to be synonymous with the psychosocial framework and the developmental perspective to be synonymous with the sociobiological framework. From the standpoint of African Americans, the developmental perspective is the most appropriate one for analyzing and devising strategies to engage in systems-centered prevention.

It is equally important for the African American community to devise an operational agenda around which systems-centered prevention activities can be measured. In this regard, Table 5 in the Appendix offers a social development model as such an agenda.

On the assumption that social development occurs best in communities that hold human values paramount, place the maintenance of life and improvement of the quality of life as ultimate goals, and view people as subjects of the world. As such, they must be considered capable of acting upon and changing the world and, in the process, contributing to the betterment of humankind. Accordingly, the following social development goals are fundamentally essential:

1. The eradication of social and economic injustice due to discrimination based on ideology, religion, race, sex, class, and ethnicity.
2. The elimination of hunger, disease, and violence, since these are absolute threats to physical survival, and the introduction of prevention as the cornerstone for action versus reaction after the fact.
3. The creation of participatory mechanisms (a political system that ensures every person an equal opportunity with every other person to influence the decisions which affect his/her life).
4. The adoption of a policy of relative self-reliance which makes maximum use of resources, both human and material, available in a community and which balances technology transfer and importation according to developmental stages.
5. The commitment to the elimination of any and all violations of human rights to ensure that no one loses opportunities to pursue life in a manner calculated to promote personal dignity.
6. The removal of illiteracy from the social fabric of the community and the organization, operation, and maintenance of educational systems which develops the fullest potential of every societal member within his/her capabilities, so that education no longer serves the role of societal stratification but, instead, of social unification.

7. The construction of decent, safe, and sanitary housing for all.
8. The creation of the necessary infrastructures—water, sewage systems, roads, communications, transportation, etc.—supportive of maximum human capacity.
9. A view of family as the crucible in which personal and societal well-being is generated and, therefore, should be accorded the requisite respect and support necessary for the effective implementation of its crucial responsibilities.
10. The development of policies which keep population growth in balance with community capacity to meet the needs of community members.
11. A respect for the non-material needs of community members as these are reflected in various religious preferences, forms, and practices.

At the most basic level of implementation, drawing upon the analytical framework of the sociobiological or developmental perspective, and guided by the outcomes sought in the social development operational agenda, each African American congregation can move forward with prevention at both levels, person-centered and systems-centered.

Prescription for greater church involvement

It is recommended that each African American congregation draw a circle one mile in diameter around its physical location and commit itself to achieving the goals herein specified. Where there is more than one church within the same one-mile area, then the ministers of the affected churches should collaborate in carrying out the necessary programs of action and prevention.

If this is done all across the United States, with the African American church taking the lead, then most assuredly, the freeway to prison that far too many African American males are traveling will be permanently interrupted.

My conclusion is expressed by a poem, "We Know This Place," written by Lucille Clifton.

> We have been on this piece of ground longer than the government. We know this place. We have walked it and worked it, fought its wars and filled its factories. We know this place. We have learned it the hard way, the blood way, the lesson that lasts, America cannot surprise us. We know this place. We bear responsibility for what we know.
>
> We are the family of tribes. The new people. We live across the whole face of this country. We are urban and rural and suburban. We speak all its languages. We know its secrets. We are its secrets.
>
> We have survived. We do survive. We are the children of the ones they could not kill. Our presence confirms us. The question now is not: Will there be an us? The question now is: What kind of us will there be? Today is the name of possibility. Today contains the traces of the past and the seeds of tomorrow. Tomorrow is vision or illusion.
>
> We must choose vision! One of the functions of the present is to dream the vision of the future from the memory of the past. Remember the love of our grandmothers. Remember it for our grandchildren. We know that we can be better than we are. Even the best of us. We are responsible for what we know.

Here is the name of the place where we must begin to accept, to embrace that responsibility. Now is the name of when we must begin. The present is the last name of the past and the first name of the future. The present is what we are in. Let us be!

REFERENCES

Clifton, Lucille. July 1976. "We Know This Place." *Essence Magazine.* New York, NY, p. 53.

King, Louis. 1989. "Comparison of Elements of Developmental and Deficit Paradigms." Fanon Center, Drew Medical School, UCLA.

Lawrence, Gary. 1990. "Attributes of Successful Black Men." Working Paper, Virginia Commonwealth University.

Lincoln, C. Eric Lincoln. Summer 1971, "The Negro Colleges and Cultural Change." *Daedalus,* 606.

APPENDIX

*Table 1: Operational Paradigm for Black Male
Survival, Redemption, and Transcendence**

Knowledge Base	Skills Bases	Value Bases	Transmission Technique
Political Economy—To understand that economic decisions are equivalent to political decisions, and political decisions are equivalent to economic decisions. There is no dichotomy between the two—they are inseparable. As such, an understanding of the construct and concept of	Analysis of micro-economic issues Analysis of macro-economic issues Ability to conceptualize the relationship between political decisions and their economic translation in the lives of African Americans. Techniques of resource aggregation, capital formation,	Relative economic self-sufficiency is a fundamental prerequisite to personal and collective freedom. Economic well-being is viewed as an essential component of community well-being. Resource procurement can never be attained at the cost of personal,	Watch TV shows which focus on the economy. Read the *Wall Street Journal* Visit banks Open up savings and checking accounts Buy stocks Spend time with mentors in business-related activities. Bridge theory and practice Involve in market surveys

political economy is imperative in a society where such decisions are rarely, if ever, made with the health, welfare, and development of Black men as a primary consideration.	and differential investment schemes (feasibility studies) Ability to establish alternative economic development paradigms in the African American community inclusive of, but not limited to, LDC's and investment clubs. Management techniques	group, and community health and viability, e.g., drugs can't be a vehicle for economic security Personal wealth is an extension of collective wealth. You don't rip off your own people. Community investment and reinvestment Use self as instrument for the economic development of others, e.g., job creation Don't ask the enemy for money to free self.	Create mock models of various economic development schemes, dialogue and discuss. Review state of Black America by National Urban League. Engage in African American community business and economic patronage. Discuss waste and extravagance. Reinforce in home, school, and community.

*The tables in this essay were developed by Dr. Creigs Beverly and may not be duplicated or used in any way without his express permission.

SPIRITUALITY

Table 2: Operational Paradigm for Black Male
Survival, Redemption, and Transcendence*

Knowledge	Skills	Values	Transmission Techniques
Spirituality in the context employed extends far beyond the notion of religion and its secular transition into denominational domains. Rather, as employed, it is deeply rooted in the concept of soul-force as developed by Leonard E. Barrett in his book of a similar title (*Soul-Force: African Heritage in Afro-American Religion*).	Living in harmony with rather than in opposition to the universal order of things. Ability to get quiet enough to get in touch with the genuineness within oneself. In using *soul force* as an instrument of liberation.	Belief in perseverance in the midst of oppression. Belief in a Supreme Being to answer the persisting question of "what do you do when there is nothing else to do?" Belief in the power of one's own "Soul-force" and that of African Americans.	Sit and be quiet at least 30 minutes a day. Take tours into the wilderness and observe nature. Study other cultures and religions other than Occidentalism. Dialogue and discuss the use of Soul-Force as an instrument of liberation both personal and communal.

"Soul-force" in "Black Talk" describes that quality of life that has enabled Black people to survive the horrors of their "diaspora." The experience of slavery, and its later repercussions, still remain to be dealt with, and "Soul" signifies the moral and emotional fiber of the Black man that enables him to see his dilemmas clearly and at the same time encourages and sustains him in his struggles. "Force" connotes strength, power, intense effort, and a will to live. The combined words—"soul force"— described the racial inheritance of the	The ability to see beyond the "is" and envision the "ought." In the arts of meditation and prayer. Translating biblical teachings into use based upon current laughter and defeat into victory. It is patience, objective reality. Effective use of range of human emotions.	Belief in the inherent dignity of all African Americans. Belief in the concept "where there is a will, there is a way, and if there is no way, find one or make one."	Read books on personal and communal transformations. Observe and record empirical evidence of Soul-Force at work. Become attached to a church and help to mold it into a community development agency.

New World
African; it is
that which
characterizes
his lifestyle, his
worldview and
his endurance
under conflict.
It is his frame of
reference vis-à-vis
the wider world
and his blueprint
for the struggle
from bondage
to freedom.
Soul-force is
that power of
the Black man
which turns
sorrow into joy
while suffering,
determination
while frustrated,
and hope while
in despair.
It derives its
impetus from the
ancestral heritage
of Africa, its
refinement from
the bondage
of slavery, and
its continuing
vitality from
the conflict of
the present.

It expresses itself collectively as well as through charismatic leaders. In addition, it can express itself in states of acquiescence, avoidance, and separation. So there is no end to the permutations and combinations of the restless "soul." Soul is visceral rather than intellectual, irrational rather than rational; it is art rather than logic			

*The tables in this essay were developed by Dr. Creigs Beverly and may not be duplicated or used in any way without his express permission.

*Table 3: Operational Paradigm for Black Male
Survival, Redemption, and Transcendence**

Family Roles and Responsibilities

Knowledge	Skills	Value Bases	Transmission Techniques
Family Roles and Responsibilities: to know the various roles, responsibilities, and tasks associated with family life. To understand the relationship between one's own family and the collective family of all African Americans. To understand and appreciate the range of family forms and structures. To know that the family is the source to both personal and communal strength.	Adult male/female relationships Child/parent relationships Husbandry Surrogate parenting Parenting (responsible) Cultivation of extended family Execution of multiple family roles Negotiating family conflict at every interactional level (peacefully) Solidarity building Protecting family from internal as well as external enemies	Absolute respect for African American women Absolute respect for elders Belief in the power of Black love Absolute respect for family life Belief in human versus material values Power at whatever level is viewed as an instrument for self, family, and communal development, never for self-exaltation, depreciation, oppression, or degradation of others.	Opportunities to play all family roles in childhood, e.g., provider, protector, nurturer, conflict resolver, educator. Establish rites of passage in the home, school, community, and church based upon the specific completion of development. Opportunities to observe and participate with males in multiple roles and functions, e.g., going to work with different men.

To understand the requirements of family solidarity. To be cognizant of the multilevel attacks on African life both internationally and domestically. To know and understand that without strong African families, there can be no strong individuals, nor a strong African Nation.	Providing territorial security Providing nurturing family environment for all members Providing spiritual guidance Guiding, directing, and counseling Planning and development Establishing boundaries Familial complementary between home, school, and community. In letting go Communications (all levels)	Absolute resistance to all forms of family violence Belief in family cooperation To always use oneself for the protection, preservation, and development of African family life, both personal, communal, and internationally. To protect against all infringement.	Opportunities to observe and participate with females in multiple roles and functions, e.g., going to work with different women. Opportunities to learn to save early in life and have a long-term plan for self, family, and community. Engage in carrying out various community service projects, e.g., renovations of homes, escorting old people, working with children, patrolling neighborhoods, etc. Use of every interactional modality to teach.

			Courses in male responsibility and family life. Rejection of Eurocentric models of maleness (seek harmony versus control).

*The tables in this essay were developed by Dr. Creigs Beverly and may not be duplicated or used in any way without his express permission.

*Table 4: Operational Paradigm for Black Male
Survival, Redemption, and Transcendence**

History and Ancestry

Knowledge	Skill Bases	Value Bases	Transmission Techniques
History and ancestry: It has been stated repeatedly that a people ignorant of their history is a people doomed to extinction. Black men must know who they are, from whence they came; their particular and special gifts; their place in the world history and their forever more. This knowledge can only be achieved if Black men become serious students of African history and the history of Africans in the diaspora.	Geography/ political history, geopolitics Discovery of the new and qualitatively different Construction of genealogy trees Separating fact from friction Transcending Eurocentric decadence Extricating oneself from the "belly of western whales" Information aggregation, conceptualization, and dissemination Reading and writing Verbal communications	Africa is the mother without qualification of all African Americans. -History gives meaning to the past, clarify on the present and give direction for the future. -Perpetual commitment to the serious study of Africa as a continent and to all her souls wherever they are in the diaspora. Promotion of African and African American culture at every level.	Demand an accurate and informed curriculum in African and African American institutions in which we participate. Travel to African countries Visit African embassies in the United Nations. Invite African and African American historians to speak.

They must know that all they are now is the product of cumulative experiences, the good, the bad, and the ugly. But more importantly, they must know that they are descendants of proud peoples, courageous peoples, inventors, doctors, scientists, warriors, navigators, builders, farmers, prophets, educators, and goldsmiths.	Historical analyses Construction of Afrocentric paradigms Seeing what is not shown, hearing what is not said, speaking what is unspoken, touching the invisible, knowing what is not known, and doing what has not been done. In being men of history, historymakers and not simply men made by history.	Commitment never to become a burden to Africa and African history, rather, an instrument of its transmission.	Treat African and African American history as a 365-day-a-year priority. Engage in systematic dialogue, discussion, reading, viewing, and listening of relevant materials. Acknowledge, celebrate, and honor all appropriate holidays and rituals.

*The tables in this essay were developed by Dr. Creigs Beverly and may not be duplicated or used in any way without his express permission.

*Table 5: Operational Paradigm for Black Male
Survival, Redemption, and Transcendence**

International Affairs and Responsibilities

Knowledge	Skill Bases	Value Bases	Transmission Techniques
International affairs and relations: To understand that spaceship earth is small and that what happens in one part of the world affects directly or indirectly every other part of the world. To understand this relationship, most especially in relation to people on the African Continent and people of African descent.	The ability to analyze the relationship between American foreign policy and the domestic welfare of African Americans. The ability to conceptualize and execute international (both bilateral and multilateral) relations with people of color worldwide.	The fate of African Americans is tied to Africans everywhere. International collaboration and cooperation between African people is requisite to overall development, redemption, and transcendence. Domestic cooperation among African Americans is a prerequisite for international cooperation. African and	Visit the United States. Visit other African countries. In-depth study in geography of the African continent. Bring in African speakers— school, church, community, etc. Read international reports such as *United Nations News*, Annual Report of USAID, the London *Economist*, etc. Visit African embassies.

To know that the elimination of Africans in any part of the world is only one step away from eliminating Africans everywhere else. To know and understand that Pan-Africanism is one of only a few means left to humanize the world. To know that the African family extends from neighborhoods in Detroit to every other neighborhood, whether in the diaspora or in Mother Africa.	Ability to aggregate data and develop predictive indicators for Black life, nationally and internationally, for proactive planning and development rather than reactivism. Analysis and observation of the operations of the United Nations, World Bank, International Monetary Fund, Club of Rome, and the Trilateral Commission. Vigilance Information aggregation and dissemination.	African American culture must be respected, promoted, and protected at every level of existence. Black life everywhere is valuable and must be preserved, protected, and promoted. If you're only for yourself, who will be for you; if not now, when!	Write an essay on international affairs (emphasis on Africa). See documentaries on Africa. See relevant movies on Africa. Engage in African and African American exchange programs. Consider international careers.

QUESTIONS FOR STUDY
AND DISCUSSION

1. Dr. Creigs Beverly describes "person-centered prevention" and "systems-centered prevention."
2. Are they inherently contradictory?
3. What are the advantages and disadvantages of each?
4. Ask the group to list attributes of a prison prevention model that might include both approaches.
5. Examine each of the ten attributes which Lawrence Gray's research indicates are present in the lives of successful Black men in the United States. Postulate the opposite of each of them and discuss what can be done by the church and society to prevent the opposite factors from influencing the development of Young African American males.
6. What is meant by the term "Rites of Passage"? Ask the group to give some examples of such "rites" in their own families or the families of others they know.
7. Let the group take as much time as it needs to review carefully the five tables Dr. Beverly has designed to diagram the content, processes, bases, and transmission techniques of Black male *survival, redemption, and transcendence.*
8. First, examine the meaning of the last three words and make sure they are understood in the group.
9. Examine the meaning of "operational paradigm." Then have group members read across the page to see the theoretical connections and evaluate the usefulness of this detailed program for ending the endangerment of young Black men in this society.

10. Are these recommendations implementable by a local congregation? What are the "helping factors" and the "hindering factors" in the role and function of our traditional congregations in relation to what Beverly is advocating in these tables? What changes are necessary in terms of how we view the church and how we strategize its outreach to persons inside and outside the congregation?

11. Have the group read what the author has to say about systems-centered prevention and then go back and read the epigraph by C. Eric Lincoln.

12. What does he mean by the statement that human possibility is a function of the interplay between time, place, and circumstance?

13. If it is true, what are the implications for systems—the government, economy, education, criminal justice, arts, religion, family, etc.?

14. Discuss and evaluate the "sociobiological" perspective. Why does Louis King insist that the developmental perspective is the most appropriate one for analyzing and devising strategies for engaging in system-centered prevention?

15. Discuss and evaluate the eleven social development goals. The author believes that his model will help each African American congregation to involve itself in the pursuit of these goals. Does the group agree? What must be the self-understanding, training, and deployment of any congregation that would undertake responsibility for such goals in its community?

16. Ask the pastor, a social worker, and a local politician to attend the session that discusses the section "Prescription for Greater Church Involvement." They could form a panel to consider some of Dr. Beverly's recommendations. For example, has a study been made of the area "one mile in diameter" around the church? What do these experts know about the area? What are the possibilities of ecumenical collaboration in carrying church-sponsored programs of action and prevention in this area?

17. An excellent closing project for the study group would be to report the results of its discussion of Dr. Beverly's recommendations to the congregation at a worship service, concluding with a verse-speaking choir reciting Lucille Clifton's poem "We Know This Place." Afterward, pass out to those present a one-page "Evaluation and Opinion Form" to get some idea of the readiness of the congregation to begin to take the lead in blocking "the freeway to prison that far too many African American males are traveling."

Hartford Memorial Baptist Church and the Kmart Retail Corporation A Partnership in Faith-Based African American Community and Social Development: A New Paradigm for the Twenty-First Century

Creigs Beverly, PhD
Wayne State University

School of Social Work

Detroit, Michigan 48202

Mangedwa C. Nyathi, MSW
Assistant to the Pastor
and Liturgist
Hartford Memorial
Baptist Church
Detroit, Michigan 48221
Phone (313) 861-1200

Eleventh International Symposium
Inter-University Consortium for International Social Development
The University of Cape Town School of Social Work
Cape Town, South Africa
July 4 through July 9, 1999

Hartford Memorial Baptist Church and the Kmart Retail Corporation
A Partnership in Faith-Based African American Community and Social Development: A New Paradigm for the Twenty-First Century

Dr. Creigs Beverly
Rev. Mangedwa C. Nyathi

Since the riots of the midsixties, many urban communities across America have experienced multiple factors leading to significant declines in the quality of urban life. Detroit, Michigan, the locus of this paper, is a typical example of one such city. Factors contributing to the decline of Detroit are inclusive of, but not limited to, Black and White middle- and upper-income family flight to the suburbs; factory/business closings and relocations; persistent problems with the quality of education provided by the Detroit Public School system; the emergence of crack cocaine and the corresponding crime it breeds; capital disinvestment and the inability of residents to get mortgage loans and business loans; excessive taxation; and a general decline in city services.

Thomas J. Sugrue (1996), in his book *The Origins of the Urban Crisis: Race and Inequality in Postwar Detroit* states:

> Detroit was America's "arsenal of democracy," one of the nation's fastest growing boomtowns and home to the highest-paid blue-collar workers in the United States. Today, the city is plagued by joblessness, concentrated poverty, physical decay, and racial isolation. Since 1950, Detroit has lost nearly a million people and hundreds of thousands of jobs. Vast areas of the city, once teeming with life, now stand abandoned. Prairie grass and flocks of pheasants have re-claimed what was, only fifty years ago, the most densely populated section of the city. Factories that once provided tens of thousands of jobs now stand as hollow shells, windows broken, mute testimony to a lost industrial past. Whole rows of small shops and stores are boarded up or burned out. Over ten thousand homes are uninhabited; over sixty thousand lots lie empty, marring almost every city neighborhood. Whole sections of the city are eerily apocalyptic. Over a third of the city's residents live beneath the poverty line, many concentrated in neighborhoods where a majority of their neighbors are also poor. A visit to the city's welfare offices, hospitals, and jails provides abundant evidence of the terrible costs of the city's persistent unemployment and poverty.

Efforts to redevelop African American communities in the United States, Detroit included, have passed through a myriad of permutations over the years. These passages have included, but have not been limited to, urban renewal, also known as urban removal, the War on Poverty; model cities; tax breaks and credits for corporations willing to operate in inner cities; a host of manpower training and employment placement programs; limited high-risk capital set aside for minority business startups; experimentation with a host of community development corporations (CDCs); enterprise zones initiated under the Bush administration; and the latest effort in the form of empowerment zones, a President Clinton initiative.

To be sure, there have been some success stories, but if one were not familiar with these developments over time historically, it would be difficult to know that they ever existed. By any objective measure one chooses to use to assess quality of life, people of African descent fare less well than nearly every other cohort in American society (Millett 1997, Sugrue 1996). This remains true not because of but in spite of a series of social experiments to correct this reality.

Through it all, the pain, doubt, fear, mistrust, suspicion and, to a great extent, the loss of hope, one institution stood out as a community anchor, a beacon, a guiding light in the midst of difficult times. The institution was and is the Black church.

As expressed by Carter (1999),

> The black church has historically been considered the heartbeat of the African American community. Largely because of the injustices faced in other institutions, early African Americans regarded the church as a refuge and believed it was the only institution that belonged   entirely to their community (Boyd-Franklin, 1989). Within the church, black Americans experienced family support, respect that was not determined solely by socioeconomic status, affirmation of their unique attributes, and immediate retribution for wrongful acts. Black churches were very important during the civil rights struggle. They aided the development of political leaders such as Nat Turner, Richard Allen, Adam Clayton Powell, Jr., Martin Luther King, Jr., Malcolm X, and Jesse Jackson.

> The church and community continue to be highly integrated, and religious practices of the church often affect other areas of community life.

Perhaps the missing link in many of these development initiatives has been the underutilization of the African American church (Billingsley 1995). The African American church is the one institution that Black people have true control over and the one institution which can move and act relatively autonomously. The African American church is also the greatest available vehicle for sustainable community development.

This paper describes a partnership created between Hartford Memorial Baptist Church and the Kmart Corporation of America to open a 24/7 Kmart retail outlet in the city of Detroit, Michigan.

This is a model for African American community development grounded in a faith-based ideology, consistent with and necessary for twenty-first-century development needs (Brauer 1997).

There are perhaps many definitions of "faith-based development." For purposes of this paper, it is defined within the fullest meaning of the construct Soul Force. To understand the concept of faith-based development, it is first necessary to understand the concept of Soul-Force. Barrett (1974) describes Soul force as

> that quality of life that has enabled black people to survive the horrors of their "diaspora." The experience of slavery and its later repercussions still remain to be dealt with; and "Soul" signifies the moral and emotional fiber of the Black man that enables him to see his dilemmas clearly and at the same time encourages and sustains him in his struggles. "Force" connotes strength, power, intense effort and a will to live. The combined words—"Soul-Force"—describe the racial inheritance of the New World African; it is that which characterizes his lifestyle, his world view and his endurance under conflict. It is his frame of

reference vis-à-vis the wider world and his blueprint for the struggle from bondage to freedom.
Soul-force is that power of the Black man which
turns sorrow into joy, crying into laughter, and
defeat into victory. It is patience while suffering,
determination while frustrated and hope while in
despair. It derives its impetus from the ancestral
heritage of Africa, its refinement from the bondage of slavery, and its continuing vitality from the
conflict of the present. It expresses itself collectively as well as through charismatic leaders. In
addition, it can express itself in states of acquiescence, avoidance, and separation. So, there is no
end to the permutations and combinations of the
restless "soul."

Definition of Faith-Based Development

Faith-based development within the context of African
American life is a model of community development rooted in the
historical experiences of African American people and the role the
Black church has played in these experiences. It is development which
takes the collective strengths, resources, both human and material
and, most importantly, the religious faith of Black people and turns
these assets into goods and services so desperately needed in African
American communities. It is activated *Soul Force.*

Faith-based community development does adhere to fundamental principles of generic community development, e.g., feasibil-
ity studies, cost-benefit analysis, capitalization, market forces, mar-
keting, amortization schedules and demands, and so forth. But the
fundamental difference is a belief that faith without works is nonpro-
ductive. Finding a way or making one when need is great provides a
level of commitment not commonly found in the open market. As
Pastor Adams of Hartford Memorial Baptist church once stated, "If
75% of the economics make sense for the project, then prayer will

guide us to find a way to make the other 25% make sense." *Faith-based development* ultimately is a combination of secular realities woven into spiritual covenants.

Brief History of Hartford

One of the major Black church anchors in Detroit during historically turbulent times and a current community beacon is the Hartford Memorial Baptist Church. Hartford is entering its eighty-second year of existence. Its founding pastor was the Reverend Edgar Wendell Edwards (1917–1920), who left Hartford to go to Chicago in 1920. After a diligent search, the church called the Reverend Charles A. Hill Sr., assistant to the Reverend Robert L. Bradby Sr. of Detroit's Second Baptist Church. Installed as pastor in November of 1920, Dr. Hill remained pastor until his retirement on his seventy-fifth birthday, April 25, 1965. During his long progressive pastorate, all the former physical facilities on the corner of Hartford and Milford were built and dedicated. Dr. Hill was an outspoken champion of civil rights in the difficult days before the Civil Rights Movement of 1955 and onward. He was one of the first Blacks to run for Detroit City Council and courageously opened the Hartford pulpit to such nonconformists as W. E. B. DuBois and Paul Robeson. A strong supporter of organized labor, UAW Ford Local 600 was organized in Hartford Church.

On April 6, 1969, Hartford gleefully received its son, Charles Gilchrist Adams, as pastor of the church in which he had been reared, indoctrinated, baptized, licensed, ordained, and married. Dr. Adams, honors graduate of University of Michigan and Harvard Divinity School, had begun his seventh year as pastor of historic Concord Baptist Church in Boston, New England's largest African American congregation. Under his strong and vigorous leadership, the old mortgage was burned in 1971, and with a growing church family, Hartford made one of the largest ecclesiastical facilities purchases in the history of Detroit on James Couzens. Hartford marched into the "new" church on April 10, 1977, burning its mortgage in 1983, nine years ahead of time.

Dr. Adams's vision of community outreach led to the establishment of AGAPE (love) house for charitable and community ministries. Housed in properties purchased across the freeway on James Couzens, AGAPE House offers needed social services such as medical referrals, free clothing, daily senior citizens program, hunger task force, bookstore, taping ministry, and scholarship and college preparation programs, KAFO and KENTAKE Academies for boys and girls, public health consortium, legal referrals, child visitation program for incarcerated mothers, W.I.C. Program, Telefriend Latchkey Program, Narcotics Anonymous, Alcoholics Anonymous, REACH Program for AIDS awareness, education and support, and the Hartford Economic Development Foundation.

Hartford has continued to purchase real estate along Seven Mile Road and James Couzens. These real estate acquisitions have led to the establishment of additional outreach ministries such as a Head Start Agency, tutorial programs, Hartford Family Program (Fathers and Mothers in League with Youth Against Drugs), OASIS Motivation Program for High Schoolers, and the Hartford Institute for Biblical Studies.

It was through the Hartford Development Foundation that the long and often difficult process to partner with the Kmart corporation in the creation of a Super Kmart 7/24 (seven days a week / twenty-four hours a day) was initiated.

History of the Kmart Corporation

Archival data from the Kmart Corporation indicates that a new concept in merchandising backed by thousands of dedicated men and women changed the S. S. Kresge Company from a fledgling newcomer in the variety-store field to a multibillion-dollar chain of general merchandise and specialty retail stores.

In 1899, Sebastion Spewing Kresge opened his first store in downtown Detroit. By 1912, Kresge had eighty-five stores with annual sales of more than $10 million. Kresge stores appealed to shoppers with the stores' low prices, open displays, and convenient locations.

Inflation in the World War I era forced Kresge to raise prices to twenty-five cents, and in the mid-twenties, Kresge opened "green-front stores" to sell items at a dollar or less, often next to the red-front dime stores.

Kresge went into the first suburban shopping center—Country Club Plaza in Kansas City, Missouri—in 1929. By 1930, variety-store chains had become commonplace because they provided a wide array of goods at low prices. Meanwhile, supermarket chains were introducing the public to self-service shopping.

The Kresge Company launched its newspaper advertising program in the early 1930s. Radio promotions followed twenty years later, and television was added in 1968. Today, print ads still dominate Kmart's advertising program with 72 million circulars weekly for insertion in 1,500 newspapers nationwide.

With the opening of America's first discount store in 1953, a new era in retailing had dawned. The Ann and Hope Mill Outlet in Rhode Island, which manufactured tinsel and corsage ribbons, sold discounted ribbons and greeting cards as well as women's housedresses for $2.19 each. Several over discount houses emerged in the 1950s, leading Kresge President Harry B. Cunningham to study a similar strategy for his organization. The result was the opening of the first Kmart discount department store in Garden City, Michigan, in 1962.

In Kmart's first year of operation, corporate sales topped $483 million. By 1966, Kresge registered it first billion-dollar year with 162 Kmart stores in operation. Kmart's 1994 sales topped 34 billion. The name of the company was changed to Kmart Corporation in 1977 to reflect the fact that more than 95 percent of sales were generated by Kmart stores. Today, there are more than 2,100 Kmart stores in the United States, Puerto Rico, Guam, and the US Virgin Islands.

Kmart employs some 265,000 individuals worldwide. Store management teams are responsible for the profitability of their own units and have the authority to make certain independent decisions about their operations. The corporation continues to expand and grow its domestic and international markets.

Inner City Market Rediscovered

Inner-city communities, long neglected and suffering from multiple negative factors impacting the quality of urban life have in recent years been, in a sense, rediscovered as viable economic markets. Some economists have even suggested that inner cities are perhaps emerging as the hottest untapped market. Roberts (1998), points out that:

> The inner city may be emerging as the hottest untapped market. After decades of alarming indicators—rising crime, dwindling population, plummeting income and education levels—the depressing trends have begun to rebound. Since 1994, famed Harvard Business School management guru Michael Porter, through his nonprofit Initiative for a Competitive Inner City, has been establishing the dollars-and-cents case for inner-city investments by corporate America. In a new study, he estimates that the inner-city retail market totals $100 billion a year. "The inner city represents the largest emerging retail market in the United States," he says, "and in many inner-city areas, more than 25 percent of retail demand is unmet."

Given these insights/new discoveries if you will, more and more attention as well as support is being given to the use of community-based organizations as inner-city redevelopment entities. Neighborhood development is economic development for everyone, reaching all the way down to the street level instead of lining the pockets of corporate executives and real estate magnates (Tobocman and Greenberg 1998).

Tobocman and Greenberg go on to state that:

> Community based development organizations have proven to be effective in the redevelopment in cities across America. Operating much like mall managers, these organizations implement community policing, recruit small businesses, promote local shopping and address other barriers to economic development, thus creating jobs and increasing tax revenues. Moreover, they understand the commercial services needed to nurture residential development, a key component of a real renaissance.

Herbert (1998) indicates that:

> For years, small neighborhood organizations, known as community development corporations, or CDCs, have been building or renovating housing that can be afforded by families of very modest means. This new housing has been a stabilizing influence in inner-city neighborhoods across the country, a defense against onrushing blight. As the neighborhoods stabilize, new families are drawn to them, creating a viable potential market in areas that previously were economically moribund. "The obvious next step is to take a look at where the families are going to shop," said Jefferson Armistead, a vice president with the Local Initiatives Support Corp. (LISC), a national organization that helps arrange funding and provides expert assistance to CDCs.

Evolution of the Partnership

The confluence of economics, time, vision, need, ministerial and service outreach made possible the evolution of the Hartford Memorial Baptist Church and the Kmart Corporation partnership.

In 1990, Hartford Memorial Baptist Church began the initial phase of a socio-economic, faith-based experiment to acquire property on Seven Mile and Meyers Roads in Northwest Detroit with a review of the property and negotiations with the owner, Grace Hospital. This thirteen-acre parcel would eventually become the future site of a proposed Super Kmart shopping center.

Four years later in 1994, half of the property was purchased. Once acquired, the church hired an environmental testing company to perform extensive environmental testing of the soil for toxic substances, etc.

The road to completion of this economic development project did not run smoothly. Hartford Memorial Baptist Church was still handicapped after 1994 because the other one-half of the property was still in negotiation. Hartford Memorial Baptist Church waited in anticipation for the time when the hospital would sell the other half of the land.

Negotiation for the property extended over a six-year period from 1990 to 1996. The other half of the property was finally acquired in December 1996.

Simultaneous with efforts to secure all of the land, Hartford began to explore potential ideas for development of the site. Request for proposals were mailed out which resulted in five prospective co-developers submitting concepts. Each co-developer was invited in for an interview with members of the Hartford Development Foundation. One co-developer, Walker, Soebel, and their associates was chosen because their plan reflected a use of the land which would be progressive, creative, and enterprising. Their proposal was for a Super Kmart shopping center and two restaurants.

Whether by historical accident or divine intervention, Kmart's search for an appropriate city of Detroit site to open a new store and

Hartford's acquisition of the land merged at an opportune time for both entities.

When Hartford Memorial Baptist church acquired this property, it had "no plans" in terms of specifically how the land would be utilized. (It was not in the church's vision at the time of acquisition that a shopping center should be built on this site.) Hartford Memorial became a risk-taker in this venture because substantial dollars were tied up in this project. As a result of this collaboration with Kmart, the church, therefore, broadened its role in community development, spiritual development, and economic development. (The church already had a significant presence in the community with its involvement in community outreach.) The church now recognized needs beyond the spiritual. The church would bring to the community a project that would

- Provide new jobs for 400–500 people;
- Provide adequate, accessible, affordable retail to citizens;
- Bring new tax revenues to improve city services consisting of $400,000 annually in real estate taxes; $125,000 in income taxes;
- $1.5 million annually in sales taxes; and
- Support public education.

Hartford Memorial Baptist Church insisted that development of this project would be conducted in a manner that would be different from that of the suburbs. As a result, Kmart Corporation held over thirty meetings with community residents. The church further insisted that there would be a consensus as well as an understanding of the development phase of the project.

Nonetheless, approximately 12–13 families could not be convinced that this project was positive for the community. These families remained opposed to the project.

An excerpt from testimony given by Della McGraw Goodwin to the City Planning Commission of Detroit on September 10, 1998, is illustrative of opposition expressed to the project by some community residents.

Mr. Chairman and members of the City Planning Commission, the Community Association of Block Clubs has expressed its opposition to the Hartford/Kmart development at West Seven Mile and Meyers Road since May of 1996. Our opposition is based on the threat of this development to the public health and safety of residents and business guests.

We have participated in all opportunities given us to reassert that the development sits at the front door of some of Detroit's most desirable housing stock. The residential neighborhood is home to many of Detroit's most educationally prepared and economically able citizens.

This incompatible, life threatening, heavy commercial project was placed before the City Council in the Sheila Cockrell ordinance, Number 15-97 on May 29, 1997. It was adopted in an 8 to 1 vote.

As advisors to the City Council on this project, you first recommended a 16-hour operation with one restaurant. You later decanted and submitted two options. We remain hopeful that Hartford and its partners will "feel the pain" of its neighbors and reduce its hours of operation.

Tonight, we thank you for your good faith efforts. Indeed, it was the work of CPC staff that changed the physical plant of Kmart to one that blends more acceptably with the $90–$ 100,000 homes on fronting streets. While this Hearing is specific to the Perkins Restaurant proposal, management of the site in its entirety must be addressed.

Before the same body a year earlier (February 20, 1997), Rev. Charles Adams spoke eloquently to the need for the project.

Rev. Dr. Charles Adams, Hartford Memorial Baptist Church, noted the events leading up to the proposed development. In the language of Swahili, he urged "let's all pull together." Dr. Adams's remarks focused on the opportunity for economic benefits and new visions for the city. Quoting scripture, Shakespeare, and William Julius Wilson Jr., Dr. Adams noted the importance of the commercial reconstruction of the neighborhood and the creation of jobs. No private dwellings will be destroyed. The city lacks retail. Dr. Adams cited the experience, reputation, and financial soundness of the co-developers. The development represents a positive social change. The aesthetics will be superior. Traffic can be rerouted and managed. The project will be successful through the cooperation of the developers and the community. As to why the community was not initially consulted, Dr. Adams noted that "talk is cheap." Since December 1996, twelve meetings have been held to work out details and address concerns. Dr. Adams felt that concentration on only the restaurants would not result in a strong financial development. Dr. Adams cited written support of Rev. Wendell Anthony, Elder Dr. Wetherly, and two thousand letters of support from individuals and other entities. Kmart will create 400–500 new jobs, raise $125,000 in income taxes and $1.5 million in sales tax.

Continuing efforts to address the concerns of community residents were made. There were several aspects involved in the development of this project. Initially, there were significant modifications to the building's design. Landscaping was utilized in a manner that would "soften" the impact of the building's presence in the community. This Super Kmart structure would not be a conventional building. It would be a structure that would have more urban character than a "square box"—more variation in design and representative of a building with old architecture rather than a "slab building."

Another aspect of this project involved what the church's position was relative to hiring practices. Hartford Memorial wanted the people of the community to be assured that those who lived in the community would be hired by Super Kmart to work in their community. The agreement was that four to five hundred community residents would receive jobs at this shopping center.

The church worked as a partner with Kmart Corporation in the hiring process. In the initial hiring phase of the project, the church opened its doors to become a temporary employment center for applicants. The Northwest Activity Center, which was located nearby, became the second temporary employment site. Over 3,200 citizens of the City of Detroit applied at this site. Of that number, over 1,200 were qualified. Again, the church recognized the importance of gaining community support. An additional way of gaining that support was to make it convenient for residents to apply for jobs. The developer brought this project to the community on terms and conditions that would make it more palatable to the community (Nyathi 1998).

It is important to note that this collaborative effort with Hartford Memorial Baptist Church and Kmart Corporation has had an impact on faith-based organizations both nationally and locally. Organizations other than faith-based organizations have been impacted as well. For example, the Northwest Advisory Committee was formed to further assure that this collaboration between Kmart and the community continues to be a success.

Kmart Corporation encouraged the Northwest Business Association through its recognition of how the Super Kmart would bring economic vitality to other area businesses as well. The presence of the shopping center would result in enhancement and improvement of their economic status as well. This helped to overcome a (negative) perception by businesses. Businesses in the area were of the mindset that Kmart would not lend them assistance and would only take away from their businesses (Walker 1998).

The City of Detroit will be in competition with the suburbs. People now leave the city and shop in the suburbs for basic needs. The (implied) intent is that they leave the city to shop in the suburbs for basic needs (limited items), but in reality, they shop for all items outside the City of Detroit.

The Northwest Advisory Committee anticipated meeting with store management on a monthly basis. The Northwest Advisory Committee will be the eyes and ears of the community. They will be the liaison between the community and Kmart. Their purpose is to assure that there will not be a lack of communication in areas where there may be potential problems. For example, the Northwest Advisory Committee will act as "mystery shoppers." They will report to the store management on the treatment of customers. For example, if a Kmart associate (employee) is not professional in the treatment of a shopper, it will be reported. Similarly, if the treatment of a customer is excellent, it will also be reported. The committee will keep a watchful eye (Nyathi 1998).

Hiring and promotion in the store will be tied to reports received from the "mystery shoppers." Community input from the Northwest Advisory Committee is also important to Kmart because Kmart wants to ensure that the level of service to customers is high.

Hartford Memorial Baptist Church will also conduct lifestyle training for employees. Lifestyle training includes things such as reporting to work on time and the treatment of customers.

The management team of the Super Kmart on Seven Mile will consist of two co-directors rather than one assistant director. One co-director is White. The other co-director is African American. The White co-director, who has had experience both with Kmart and Kroger, will train the African American co-director.

In conclusion, Kmart Corporation worked hard to make this collaboration with Hartford Memorial Baptist Church a success. The emphasis was, and is, on the best manner in which to operate this store (Walker 1995).

Perhaps the best way to sum up the impact of this project on the Detroit Community is to *quote* in its entirety an article which appeared in the *Detroit News Sunday*, November 22, 1998, entitled "Kmart's Entry Is a Big Deal in Detroit—a City in Need of Shopping Venues," written by Laura Berman.

> The new Super Kmart on Seven Mile offers neither the biggest nor the best of anything, as far as I can tell. There's no café in a rain forest, no steeply marked-down Chanel suits, no whimsical refrigerator magnet boutique. This Super Kmart on the west side is a clean, well-lighted place to

buy everyday merchandise, including car bat-
teries, Starbucks Frappuccino ice cream, minib-
linds and collard greens—but unique it is not.
Remarkable, though, it is. In our shopping-mad
culture, where we go ga-ga over a sprawling mall
in Auburn Hills, it might be easy to overlook the
significance of a store almost exactly like 100
other Super Kmarts across the nation.

What is remarkable is that a major American
city gets wildly excited about a new store that
would be a yawn elsewhere—because residents
have been driving all over the suburbs just to buy
the stuff of everyday life. On ribbon-cutting day
last Wednesday, would-be shoppers hovered outside the store's doors at Seven Mile and Meyers as
early as 7 a.m. All 800 shopping carts were in use
almost immediately, so a couple of hundred others had to be rushed over. By the time I arrived,
checkout lines wove through Martha Stewart
coordinated pillowcases and shams, all the way to
rugs and small appliances. The lines were so long
people were leaning over their carts, engaging in
long animated conversations with strangers as if
they were at a social event.

You would've thought you were in some
dinky town such as Hillsdale when the Wal-Mart
finally arrived, not in big-city Detroit. Every person I spoke to in that store currently shops in the
suburbs because nothing similar exists anywhere
near their Detroit neighborhoods.

"Ecstatic" is how Gladys Sain describes her
reaction. She lives nearby, just returned from a
trip to Cancun, Mexico, and usually shops at
Meijers in Southgate or Kmart in Dearborn.
"Why would people want to fight something like
this that's in our community, that's got excellent

merchandise, good quality, that's convenient? Why?" she asked.

I overheard a woman talking about how the store would help the city's tax base and boost economic development. "We homeowners can't afford to carry the whole tax burden. We need this," said Martha Walker, who managed a real estate office until last month.

"My wife and I have four children and we would rather shop here than in the suburbs," Steven Banks said. "We intend to spend a lot of money here and hopefully other people will too." The real fear about the store is that it's a temporary nirvana that will soon be just another dingy, rundown, second class place. "We want the best and we don't mind paying," Maggie Hardy yelled in produce.

Outside the store, a pizza truck was playing Motown hits, and two men picketed, carrying "Boycott Kmart" signs—a sentiment that makes no sense, especially once you step inside. Inside, 600 people had new jobs and thousands shopped for groceries and household goods without leaving their neighborhoods. Nothing remarkable really, unless you can't do it.

Social Development and Faith-Based Development: The Nexus

The United Nations (1995), points out the following as pertains to social development:

The ultimate goal of social development is to improve and enhance the quality of life of all people. It requires democratic institutions, respect for all human rights and fundamental freedoms, increased and equal economic opportunities, the rule of law, the promotion of respect for cultural diversity and the rights of persons belonging to minorities, and an active involvement of civil society. Empowerment and participation are essential for democracy, harmony and social development. All members of society should have the opportunity and be able to exercise the right and responsibility to take an active part in the affairs of the community in which they live. Gender, equality and equity and the full participation of women in all economic, social and political activities are essential. The obstacles that have limited the access of women to decision-making, education, health-care services and productive employment must be eliminated and an equitable partnership between men and women established, involving men's full responsibility in family life. It is necessary to change the prevailing social paradigm of gender to usher in a new generation of men and women working together to create a more humane world order.

Social development is inseparable from the cultural, ecological, economic, political and spiritual environment in which it takes place. It cannot be pursued as a sectoral initiative. Social development is also clearly linked to the development of peace, freedom, stability and security, both nationally and internationally. To promote social development requires an orientation of values, objectives and priorities toward the well-being of all and the strengthening and promotion of conducive institutions and policies. Human dignity, all human rights and fundamental freedoms, equality, equity and social justice constitute the fundamental values of all societies. The pursuit, promotion and protection of these values, among others, provides the basic legitimacy of all institutions and all exercise of authority and promotes an environment in which human beings are at the centre of concern for sustainable development. They are entitled to a healthy and productive life in harmony with nature.

The partnership between Hartford Memorial Baptist Church and the Kmart Corporation not only incorporates the principles of social development as spelled-out in the United Nations report but it also represents a substantive example of the utilization of the core principles of effective community building (National Community Building Network, 1999).

Were it not for different labels, the goals of social development articulated by the United Nations and the core principles of effective community building as articulated by NCBN would be indistinguishable.

NCBN (National Community Building Network) posits the following core principles for effective community building:

1. **Forge partnerships through collaboration.** Building community requires work by all sectors—local residents, community-based organizations, business, schools, religious institutions, health and social service agencies—in an atmosphere of trust, cooperation and respect. It takes time and committed work to make such collaboration more than rhetoric.

2. **Require racial equity**. Racism remains a barrier to a fair distribution of resources and opportunities in our society; our work promotes equity for all groups.

3. **Build on community strengths**. Past efforts to improve urban life have too often addressed community deficits; community building efforts build on local capacities and assets.

4. **Integrate development and human service strategies.**
    Traditional antipoverty efforts have separated "bricks
    and mortar" projects from those that help families and
    develop human capital; each approach needs the other to
    be successful.

5. **Foster broad community participation.** Many urban
    programs have become professionalized and alienated from
    the people they serve; new programs and policies must be
    shaped by community residents.

6. **Support families and children.** Strong families are the
    cornerstone of strong communities; community building
    efforts help families to help themselves.

7. **Value cultural strengths.** Our efforts promote the values
    and history of our many cultural traditions and ethnic
    groups.

8. **Start from local conditions**. There is no cookie cutter to
    building community; the best efforts flow from and adapt
    to local realities.

The interactional matrix which follows shows the translation
of community building principles into the more generic outcomes
associated with social development as applied in this case study.

HARTFORD MEMORIAL BAPTIST
CHURCH AND THE KMART RETAIL
CORPORATION A PARTNERSHIP IN
FAITH-BASED AFRICAN AMERICAN
COMMUNITY AND SOCIAL
DEVELOPMENT A NEW PARADIGM FOR
THE TWENTY-FIRST CENTURY
AN INTERACTIONAL MATRIX
OF COMMUNITY-BUILDING
PRINCIPLES AND SOCIAL
DEVELOPMENT OUTCOMES

	Community Building Principles	Partnership Activities	Social Development Outcomes
1.	*Forge partnerships through collaboration.* Building community requires work by all sectors—local residents, community-based organizations, business, schools, religious institutions, health and social service agencies—in an atmosphere of trust, cooperation and respect. It takes time and committed work to make such collaboration more than rhetoric.	Actively engaged local residents and businesses through a series of community forums for development input and information dissemination. Worked closely with city officials, especially the City Planning Commission, City Council, Planning and Development, Zoning and Engineering. Established employment referral systems between schools and local social service agencies.	Inclusion; maximum access and participation in a single market open to all; common interests.

| 2. | *Require racial equity.* Racism remains a barrier to a fair distribution of resources and opportunities in our society; our work promotes equity for all groups. | Hartford is a predominantly Black church with a few White members. Successful implementation of the partnership required cooperation between all groups. Kmart is primarily a White-controlled company. The mere partnership between Kmart and Hartford was organic witness to the neutralization of racism. | Equal rights and privileges; social justice; empowerment. |

3.	*Build on community strengths.* Past efforts to improve urban life have too often addressed community deficits; community-building efforts build on local capacities.	Community assets included a community with resources; a willingness to maximize their dollars by spending in their own community; a contiguous and capable workforce, availability of local contractors to help build complex; locating a mini-police precinct in the complex; hiring and promoting community residents at all levels.	People-centered sustainable development; assets; strengths based; social investment.

| 4. | *Integrate development and human service strategies.* Traditional antipoverty efforts have separated "brick and mortar": projects from those that help families and develop human capital; each approach needs the other to be successful. | The partnership focused on job development and promotion from day one. Job stratification ranged from inventory clerks to associate managers. Employment was made available to high school youth to heads of families. Efforts of the mini-police precinct were to help and refer rather than prosecute and lock up. The Kmart foundation was also instrumental in funding local community-based organizations. | Enterprise; production; assets |

5.	*Foster broad community participation.* Many urban programs have become professionalized and alienated from the people they serve; new programs and policies must be shaped by community residents.	Though there was some marginal community opposition to the project, the vast majority of residents supported the activity at all levels and their input was factored into design and construction considerations. This was especially true regarding traffic flow, security, hours of delivery, sanitation and maintenance, aesthetics, and noise abatement.	Equal standards for all groups; safe neighborhoods; institutional change to achieve growth through planning and prevention; empowerment.

| 6 | *Support families and children.* Strong families are the cornerstones of strong communities; community-building efforts help families to help themselves. | The church has nearly 10,000 members and approximately 3,000 families. Revenues from the partnership help to support a myriad of family support and development activities: emergency assistance, student scholarships, food and clothing, legal and medical services, AIDS awareness and prevention, individual and family counseling, financial management and investment seminars, Headstart Program, male and female rites of passage programs, Alcoholics Anonymous and Narcotics Anonymous, employment and training. | People-centered sustainable development; inclusion; social justice; safe neighborhoods; strengths based; social investment; empowerment. |

| 7 | *Value cultural strengths.* Our efforts promote the values and the history of our many cultural traditions and ethnic groups. | The Kmart store, in addition to offering "one stop" merchandise shopping is also sensitive to cultural likes and dislikes of area residents. These can range from certain food types (seasonal and generic) to ethnic sensitive artifacts. The store also provides an outlet for area businesses to promote their products, e.g., baked goods, seasonings, and clothing items. | People-centered sustainable development; assets; social justice; inclusion. - |

| 8 | *Start from local conditions.* There is no cookie-cutter approach to building community; the best efforts flow from and adapt to local realities. | The entire project grew out of an assessment of local shopping needs and the best way to at least, in part, address this need. After several ideations and permutations of development ideas, it was finally concluded that a "one-stop" shopping complex was needed. Hartford had the land, Kmart the model, and the rest is history. Two world-class restaurants are also on the drawing boards for the area. None currently exist in the community. | |

Social Development Outcomes were adapted from:
Mayadas, N. and Elliot D. (1998) ("Social Exclusion, Social Development and Social Work, Cairo, Egypt." Tenth IUCISD Conference.)

SUMMARY AND CONCLUSIONS

The partnership between Hartford Memorial Baptist Church and the Kmart corporation, which resulted in the construction and operation of a twenty-four-hour, seven-days-a-week comprehensive one-stop-shopping retail store in the City of Detroit is an empirical example of faith-based development at its best.

The annual revenues which will be paid to Hartford by the Kmart Corporation will help to underwrite additional community-based development initiatives. Among the future projects under consideration are a comprehensive family life development center and congregate housing for the elderly.

This revenue stream, plus the resources already inherent in the Hartford congregation will ensure a high degree of development sustainability for years to come. Sustainability, whether internationally, nationally, or locally, is deemed absolutely critical in all planning and development literature.

James, Power, Forrest and Wolfe (1999) offer a review of definitions of sustainable development. They posit that sustainable development

- is development that meets the needs of the present without compromising the ability of future generations to meet their own needs (The World Commission on Environment and Development, Our Common Future Report);
- occurs when the ecosystem, organism, or renewable resource is maintained indefinitely at a rate within its capacity for renewal (Michigan Economic and Environmental Roundtable);

- maintains or enhances economic opportunity and community well-being while protecting and restoring the natural environment upon which people and economics depend (Minnesota Legislature);
- recognizes the relationship between economic growth, environmental protection and social equity; the synergy of these goals promotes a healthy economy, a clean environment and an involved citizenry (Sustainable Coastal Communities Workshop);
- and growth is in balance with its environment, where the needs of people, creatures, land, and the economy are being met without exceeding the capacity of the land, natural resources, and supporting infrastructure and without compromising the ability of the environment to support the needs of future generations (New England Planning, November 1996).

The partnership between Hartford Memorial Baptist Church and the Kmart Corporation meets the requirements of *sustainability*. The Hartford Church has long-standing roots in the Detroit Community and the confluence of vision, skills, incentives, resources, and an action plan converted what ought to be into what is, and what is into what can be. Faith-based development is now and will continue to be a viable community and economic development model (paradigm) for the twenty-first century.

References

Barrett, Leonard. 1974. *Soul-Force: African Heritage in Afro-American Religion*. New York: Anchor Press, Doubleday, pp 1–2.

Berman, Laura. 1998, Nov. 22. "Kmart's Entry Is Big Deal in Detroit—a City in Need of Shopping Venues.

Billingsley, Andrew. 1995. "The Black Church as a Social Service Institution: Detroit." *Black Caucus Journal*, vol. 1, #4, pp 1–9.

Boyd-Franklin, N. 1989. *Black Families in Therapy*. New York: Guilford Press.

Brauer, Molly. 1997. "Kmart Digs into Detroit Location, Detroit, Michigan." *Detroit Free Press*-Section E, p. 1–2.

Carter, Carolyn S. 1999. Church Burning in African American Communities: Implications for Empowerment Practice. Social Work, pp 44, 63.

Herbert, Bob. 1998, July 7. "Retail Is Rediscovering Inner Cities." *Detroit Free Press*, p. 7a.

James, Sarah, Joe Power, Clyde Forrest, and Joshua Wolfe. 1999. "American Planning Association Draft Policy Guide on Sustainability." Lansing, Michigan, Planning and Zoning News. Vol. 17, #6, pp 5–11.

Mayadas, N. and D. Elliot. 1998. "Social Exclusion, Social Development and Social Work, Cairo, Egypt." Tenth IUCISD Conference.

Millet, R. 1997. "Evaluating Kellogg Funded Urban Initiatives. Detroit." Kellogg Foundation Inservice Training for Grantees.

National Community Building Network. 1999. "Core Principles of Effective Community Building." Oakland, CA. NCBN, p. 1.

Nyathi, M. 1998, Oct. 13. "Thoughts on the Hartford/Kmart Partnership." Detroit, Michigan.

Roberts, Johnnie L. 1998, June 15. "Touch of Magic." *Newsweek*, p. 41.

Sugure, Thomas J. 1996. *The Origins of the Urban Crisis: Race and Inequality in Post War Detroit*. Princeton, New Jersey: Princeton University Press, p. 3.

Tobocman, Steve and Marlowe Greenberg. 1998, Oct. 20. "Revive the Neighborhoods Too." *Detroit Free Press*, p. 9a.

United Nations. 1995. "Programme of Action of the World Summit for Social Development." New York: United Nations Department of Public Information-DPI-170709516294, pp 41–42.

Walker, Rick. 1998, Oct. 13. "Thoughts on the Hartford/Kmart Partnership." Detroit, Michigan.

THE BLACK CHURCH AND COMMUNITY: A MODEL FOR COMMUNITY DEVELOPMENT

Dr. Brye McMillon

From the arrival of the first African slaves to the coast of America, the pursuit of freedom and equality have been the goal of African Americans. Groups like the Free African Society founded by Richard Allen helped many reach this goal.[19] The signing of the Emancipation Proclamation should have achieved the necessary results, but it did not. Passing of the Civil Rights Act of 1964 should also have eliminated the inequalities, but it did not. Although eventually slavery met its end, African Americans continued to struggle in every area of life. The source of the continued struggle lies in the depressed social, physical, and mental state imposed upon an entire people for an extended period. This imposed environment is akin to that experienced by the children of Israel in their time of bondage in Egypt (Gen 15:13–16).

Slowly the freedoms promised by the Emancipation Proclamation began to appear, but not without a fight. Many oppressors wondered what else the Negro wanted.[20] They could not understand the magnitude of the problem, nor gauge the fire that burned

---

[19.] Robert B. Hill, "The Role of the Black Church in Community and Economic Development Activities," *National Journal of Sociology* 8, no. 1/2 (Winter94 1994): 149.

[20.] Medgar W. Evers, "The Years of Change Are Upon Us," *The Crisis*. Jun–Jul 1988, 42, accessed June 24, 2017. https://books.google.com/books?id=NwzZUpIpCsAC&pg =PA42&lpg=PA42&dq#v=onepage&q&f=false.

within Black America motivating them to pursue and achieve equality. If not equality, at a minimum, a life of comfort was the goal. Equality and comfort were represented in their minds by the elimination of a myriad of challenges.

The basic and most frustrating challenge was gaining recognition as human beings. This challenge encompasses the basic right to vote, access to and use of public facilities and services, access to educational opportunities, and fair access to employment and housing, just to name a few. The Civil Rights Act of 1964 was a welcomed relief and designed to achieve the felt needs along with the stated goals.[21] The Voting Rights Act of 1965 followed closely behind the Civil Rights Act and outlawed the prerequisite discriminatory voting practices adopted in many southern states after the Civil War.[22] Without these rights, the African American felt entrapped. This feeling spiritually left them wondering how they could connect with their spirituality in a strange land (Ps 137:4).

The passage of these laws did much for the African American people, but true equality and success were still not in their grasp. The church became the rallying point to achieve the goal of equity because of its unifying presence and basic mission of spiritual liberation. The church engaged in community development by creating housing, while their effort to support economic improvement was expressed in the creation of credit unions, cooperatives, and small businesses.[23] Because of these engagements, the African American community began to flourish.

However, something happened, and the church disengaged. This disengagement resulted in the African American Community's relapse. The spiritual degradation led to the social and moral decline of the community and individual. One aspect of this disengagement

---

[21.] U.S. Equal Employment Opportunity Commission, Title VII of the Civil Rights Act of 1964, accessed 18 April 2014. http://www.eeoc.gov/laws/statutes/titlevii.cfm.

[22.] The United States Department of Justice. The Voting Rights Act of 1965, accessed 18 April 2014. http://www.justice.gov/crt/about/vot/intro/intro_b.php.

[23.] Hill, *The Role of the Black*, Winter 94, 150.

may be attributed to deterioration of leadership in the church.[24] When leadership declined, new leaders disengaged from previous efforts. This leadership disengagement was caused by the church looking inward instead of outward.[25] The change in church focus was not a change in its belief in God or the mission of disciple making. Rather, the Black church began focusing more on those who entered its doors, seeking to "facilitate a deeper commitment among believers,"[26] while those outside the church were not being discipled, worsening the spiritual, social, and economic position of the community. The new focus of the church was misguided at best.

Consider the physical freedom of man. Throughout the Old Testament, there was a constant call for an exodus of the children of Israel from captivity. This release was physical in nature, with spiritual, emotional, and psychological implications for those involved. But for God, it was about a divine relationship. By reestablishing this connection, the church is the only agency equipped to lead the development effort to achieve spiritual and physical well-being on earth.

What Is Community Development?

Community development, regardless of the approach, can be defined as the enhancement of the community's ability to care for itself. Stated another way, community development is "the improvement of the condition of a particular area or community, especially

---

24. Knud Jorgensen, *Equipping for Service: Christian leadership in Church and Society* (Oxford: Regnum Books International, 2012), 1.
25. Amandia Speakes-Lewis, LeRoi L. Gill, and Crystal George Moses, "The Move Toward American Modernity: Empowerment and Individualism in the Black Mega Church," *Journal of African American Studies*, 15, no 2 (2011): 242.
26. Neil Cole, *Organic Church: Growing Faith Where Life Happens* (San Francisco, CA: Jossey Bass, 2005), 47.

regarding health, housing, education, etc. (frequently attributive)."[27] Alison Gilchrist also provides a more holistic definition:

> Community development represents a broad approach to working with people in communities to achieve greater levels of social justice. In the main, the focus is on individuals, groups and networks that want or need to cooperate in order to realize change at a local or community level. That change might be driven by an external threat to people's quality of life (for example, the building of new housing on much-loved green space) or it could be shaped by resident's desire to improve service for a particular section of the community (for example, providing facilities for young people to divert them from drugs or vandalism). Adopting a community development approach means ensuring that the issues and priorities are identified and agreed by the communities themselves, and that people are encouraged together toward a collective solution to a shared concern.[28]

This view of community development goes beyond simply identifying need and developing people, and rather provides a focus on equitable treatment of citizens. This idea of equitable treatment seeks to improve the economic and social standing of those within a given community, providing opportunities to pursue life's dreams.

Christian community development, however, is expressed in terms of the pursuit and mission of those carrying out this function. "The roots of the Christian Community Development movement come from a Christian worldview and perspective about how

---

[27.] *Oxford Dictionary*. s.v. "community development," accessed October 1, 2016, https://en.oxforddictionaries.com/definition/community_development.

[28.] Alison Gilchrist, *The Short Guide to Community Development* (Portland, OR: Policy Press, 2011), 2.

to respond to people living in poverty."[29] This response represents the Christian approach to reaching and addressing identified needs. These needs must be collectively agreed upon to ensure the true needs and desires of the community are being addressed and not the symptoms of these deeper needs and desires. The symptoms in this context represent what those outside of the community believe are needs without assessment and validation. One of the most pressing needs the church considers is the need for the individuals in the community to have a relationship with Christ.

The Christian community development approach is based solely on biblical principles and seeks to connect with and address man's greatest need—salvation. In this phenomenon called Christian community development, it is the local church that is the most effective in meeting the needs and bridging the gap by building effective relationships.[30] The real idea of Christian community development "is for people to be in a loving fellowship with God and with one another as they toil in fruitful labor, which benefits their community of need."[31] This benefit is spiritual but has a physical impact. When spiritual needs are met, life improves in all areas.

The History of Christian Community Development

The true history of Christian community development is biblically based. The New Testament book of Acts indicates that the church community collectively supported the physical needs of the body by selling individual assets and providing for those in need (Acts 2:45). This meeting of needs was accomplished after the church came together as a body unified in Christ. This selfless act provided food as well as accounted for all human and material needs, allowing the focus of the spiritual leaders to remain on Christ. It further conveys

---

[29.] Mackenzie Huyser and Jason Pittman., "Article Title," *Social Work & Christianity* 33, no. 4 (Winter 2006), 325–329.

[30.] Perkins, *Restoring At-Risk Communities*, 44.

[31.] Ibid, 45.

the idea that when believers connect with believers and unbelievers, they can improve the spiritual and physical life of the individual and community.

John 4 is a further example of Jesus's engagement and care for the community. After completing some of his work, Jesus identified his need to travel through Samaria. "Some think that Christ must needs go through Samaria because of the good work he had to do there; a poor woman to be converted, a lost sheep to be sought and saved. This was work his heart was upon, therefore He must needs go this way."[32] Regardless of the reason, when he arrived there, he engaged. Through His engagement, Jesus improved the spiritual disposition of the woman he met and those of whom she was connected. Jesus's engagement led to the spiritual freedom of the woman and the community, resulting in a release from physical, emotional, and psychological bondage, all things that gripped the community because of the spiritual deficiencies.

Beyond biblical times to more recent expressions of support, outreach, and commitment to community development and improvement, one can see the church has at times been intricately engaged. The church was the rallying point for the ending of slavery because of its unifying presence and the basic mission of spiritual liberation it represented and fostered. This spiritual liberation led to a belief that in God, all are equal. The church excelled, and its leadership was instrumental in the passage of the Civil Rights Act and social improvements experienced in the African American Community. These leaders understood the need to exercise a broad range of leadership skills: being imaginative, innovative, emotionally engaged, and the need to improvise. They also had the ability to organize, plan, administer effectively, and maintain order.[33]

The church engaged in community development through the creation of housing, while expressing their effort to support eco-

---

[32.] Matthew Henry, *Matthew Henry's Commentary on the Whole Bible: Complete and Unabridged in One Volume* (1934 repr. Peabody: Hendrickson, 1995).

[33.] Bob Burns, Tasha D. Chapman, and Donald C. Guthrie, *Resilient Ministry: What Pastors Told Us About Surviving and Thriving* (Downers Grove, IL: InterVarsity Press, 2013), 199.

nomic improvement in the creation of credit unions, cooperatives, and small businesses.[34] In these engagements, the church remained true to its mission of making disciples for Christ. Because of these engagements, the African American community began to flourish.

The efforts of the church in the community were far-reaching, focusing on the "social well-being of low-income neighbors or communities. Such efforts may range from community beautification to the construction of affordable housing for low-income individuals, families and seniors."[35] These efforts addressed the entire range of needs, arguably none more important than education.[36]

With the church's history of community involvement, one must wonder what occurred to stifle this engagement. One reason is clear; churches are no longer community based but comprised of members from a vast area. In other words, churches are not necessarily neighborhood institutions.

> Churches often pull people together around common ethnicity, regional or national origin, class background, political orientation, life stage, or lifestyle. Less often do congregations form around shared neighborhood identity. Many churches draw membership from a geographic area much wider than the immediate neighborhood. People pick churches according to social identity more than spatial proximity. One black congregation, then, might primarily consist of educated middle-class professionals, while another consists of working-poor people. One church may attract southern migrants, while another appeal mainly to native northerners. Another church might

---

34. Robert B. Hill, 150.
35. Ibid., 151.
36. Leak, Halima N. and Chera D. Reid. "'Making Something of Themselves': Black Self-Determination, The Church and Higher Education Philanthropy." *International Journal of Educational Advancement* 10, no. 3 (December 2010): 236.

serve Haitians or West Indians rather than blacks born in the United States.[37]

Because they are not neighborhood churches and predominantly composed of members outside of the neighborhood, churches may not be connected to or have the needs of the community at the forefront of their worship or outreach activities. To some degree and in some respects, the church has lost touch with those within its walls and those outside its walls.[38]

On another front, as alluded to earlier, the church has even overlooked those within its walls. This neglect for those within the church is related to the worship experience, leaving them spiritually and culturally irrelevant.[39] This irrelevance speaks to the watered-down gospel being preached and the distancing of the church from the community. At times, the church preaches more about wealth and conquering something than about salvation. This, added to the fact the church is no longer a microcosm of the community, leaves it culturally starved.

This turn from looking outward to looking inward prompts the question, what changed? The response is "everything changed." The church began focusing on membership and growth.[40] Society changed, the education level of members changed, socioeconomic status changed, and the very nature of community changed. The world changed. The previous isolation of countries and communities resulting from time and space has been overcome by information technology and international travel. The once limited awareness of other religions and beliefs in absolute truths has been overcome by

---

[37] Omar M. McRoberts, "Black Churches, Community and Development," Shelterforce Online. January/February 2001, accessed 15 October 2016, http://www.nhi.org/online/issues/115/McRoberts.html.

[38] Kevin G. Harney and Bob Bouwer, *U-Turn Church: New Direction for Health and Growth* (Grand Rapids, US: Baker Books, 2011), accessed November 25, 2016. ProQuest Ebrary, 7.

[39] Harney, *U-Turn Church*, 2011.

[40] Rick Rusaw and Eric Swanson, *The Externally Focused Church*. (Loveland, CO: Group Publishing, 2004), 16.

relativism.[41] People became worldlier or, at least, more aware of the world.

The church is rightfully concerned with other worldly events.[42] They are without question preaching the Gospel to the poor and leading churchgoers to spiritual freedom from captivity. As they pursue and achieve the spiritual freedoms and maturity, they should help the believer grasp how they must live out their beliefs in a sinful world. This demands helping members understand how their faith impacts and plays on their physical, social, and economic interaction and freedom. However, the church may not be positioned for effective outreach that impacts the whole person.

Churches are building larger facilities and performing major renovations on current structures. The building fund budgets are constantly expanding while outreach support budgets are all but nonexistent.

When the poor approach the church for assistance, they are met with opposition from members and pastors alike, especially if money is a part of their request. In some cases, the church's hesitation is understandable because of the frequency of requests. The cause could also potentially be attributed to the church's lack of viable programs or trained ministry teams to achieve substantive change in the life of the needy.

The church appears to benefit immensely from the community through participation in fundraising, worship attendance, and the willingness of parishioners to sacrifice when and where needed to ensure ministry occurs. This idea of ministry, however, has gotten perverted. Jesus directed the purpose and focus of ministry: "Then Jesus came to them and said, 'All authority in heaven and on earth has been given to me. Therefore, go and make disciples of all nations, baptizing them in the name of the Father and of the Son and of the Holy Spirit, and teaching them to obey everything I have commanded you. And surely, I am with you always, to the very end of the age'" (Matt 28:18–20). The proclamation to go is clear, but the

---

[41.] Neil Cole, *Church 3.0: Upgrades for the Future of the Church.* (San Francisco, CA: Wiley, 2010), 19.

[42.] Omar M. McRoberts.

church of today is sitting back, waiting for people to come. While the church waits, it fails to reach the lost, make disciples, and educate the body. Educating the body of Christ and reaching out to the lost is paramount. Scripture also highlights the necessity of education and the results for failure to educate when it addresses the importance of knowledge (Hos 4:6). Knowledge is gained through reaching and teaching.

The impact of the church sitting back is evident. The effects of the church's disengagement are seen in the ballooning of health needs in the African community with cholesterol, hypertension, heart attacks, AIDS, etc. reaching epidemic proportion.[43] Reduced numbers of African American children are completing secondary schools.

Schools in research areas (Athens City, Limestone, Lawrence, Morgan, and Madison Counties) rank from the lower to upper half of all schools in the state, with at least one school ranked 350 out of 358 among other schools in the state of Alabama.[44] Failure in secondary education means fewer students attending college and leading to fewer qualified members available to compete for positions that can positively affect the community. Poverty levels are increasing, income levels are decreasing, reliance on government subsidies is increasing, while availability of government support is at risk.

These declines in income, health, education, etc. have led to increases in areas neither the community, nor the church are proud of, most notably, incarceration. This increase in incarceration is almost a deviance being used to define a race, a community, and a people. "Because poor black men and women tend to live in racially and economically segregated neighborhoods, these neighborhoods feel the brunt."[45] Social deviance resulting in the incarceration of

---

[43] Vickie M. Mays, Susan D. Cochran, and Namdi W. Barnes, "Race, Race-Based Discrimination, and Health Outcomes Among African Americans," *Annual Review of Psychology* 58 (2007): 201–225.

[44] Trisha Powell Crain, June 18, 2013. *Alabama's High School Graduation Rates 2011–2012*. Alabama Schools Connection.org, accessed 18 April 2014. http://alabamaschoolconnection.org/2013/06/18/alabamas-high-school-graduation-rates-2011–2012/.

[45] Dorothy E. Roberts, "The Social and Moral Cost of Mass Incarceration in African American Communities." *Stanford Law Review* 56, no. 5 (2004): 1275–

African Americans appears to be a form of compensatory behavior designed to compensate for the personal impotence in a culture that perceives and responds to Black men as if they were nonpersons. The degradation of the individual in the community has also had a major impact on the church. Additionally, fewer Black men in the church has impacted its leadership and its commitment to the community.

This degradation has also had an impact on the mental state of the community. This mental degradation is further impacted because of the lack of spiritual influence of the church. Why is this important? Because spirituality impacts mental health, especially when dealing with African Americans.[46]

The church does not engage in building or repairing homes for the homeless, and the hungry that find themselves in church are still starving unless government sponsored programs are available. This was highlighted several years ago at a church meeting in Northern Alabama. When approached to provide food for the less fortunate, members proclaimed, "There are no hungry people in this area." This statement alone shows the lack of knowledge and desire to reach the less fortunate. All of this happens while Alabama is the sixth poorest state in the nation, and Blacks in the state have a poverty rate of more than 30 percent.[47] The church must reengage so that the life of Christ can be experienced in the world today. The church is the salt of the earth, but it appears this salt has lost its savor (Matt. 5:13).

These results in the above declines affected, and continue to affect, members of the church and community. Although, in cases historical like these, change is inevitable, and "in times of change, learners inherit the Earth, while the learned find themselves beautifully equipped to deal with a world that no longer exists."[48] As such,

---

1276, accessed June 1, 2017 http://www.jstor.org/stable/40040178.

[46.] Creigs Beverly, "Spirituality and Mental Health African American Men and Police, African Centered Social Work Supervision," *Journal of the National Association of Black Social Workers*, 2, No. 4 (Spring 1997), 1.

[47.] Suanne Macartney, Alemayehu Bishaw, and Kayla Fontenot, *Poverty Rates for Selected Detailed Race and Hispanic Groups by State and Place, 2007–2011. 2013.* United Census Bureau, accessed 14 April 2014. http://www.census.gov/2013pubs/acsbr11–17.pdf.

[48.] Cole, *Church 3.0*, 23.

the church had to change. The change needed was not to isolate itself; rather, the church could have benefited by inverting itself, adopting a missional theology. This phenomenon appears to be changing again. Black churches are seeking personal salvation, and this personal salvation is impacting the approach and success in every aspect of life.[49]

A more modern phenomenon can be labeled as a hybrid church, cell church, house church, or simple church.[50] These ideas of church are a trip back to the past where church was community based and a trip to the present where churches are growing and centralizing. These new small churches are community based with worshippers meeting in different locations, including individual homes. This new approach allows all the needs of the individual to be addressed by the church and ensures the church is not starved culturally. Relationships are built around a central theme—Christ. Members are then able to provide greater levels of support to and for each other. This support ensures brother cares for brother, sister cares for sister, with spiritual well-being at the forefront.

Based on the projection and research of those pursuing this model, the church of the future will be both smaller and larger.[51] In this multirole approach and size, the church will be able to revive its connection with the local community, while continuing its pursuit of world missions. This new model and focus, accompanied by a desire and awareness of the needs of the community, will lead to greater involvement and success. This greater involvement and access align with Jesus's proclamation of greater works, not flashier miracles but greater works in leading the lost to the saving Grace of Christ.[52]

[49.] Andrew Billingsley, *Mighty Like a River* (New York: Oxford Press, 1999), 87.

[50.] Dave Browning, *Deliberate Simplicity: How the Church Does More by Doing Less* (Grand Rapids: Zondervan, 2009), 1.

[51.] Ibid., 7.

[52.] Timothy Chester and Steve Timmis, *Total Church: A Radical Reshaping around Gospel and Community* (Wheaton, Ill: Crossway Books, 2008), 24.

The Process of Community Development

Some eyebrows may be raised at the idea that community development can be expressed as a process, but this is the very nature of development. Like the processes of coaching, mentoring, or counseling, there are as many approaches as there are entities engaged in the item being pursued. None of these approaches can be considered wrong if biblically based and work for the body employing them. This process, as it were, will allow the church to understand their ability to engage, its best approach, and where to engage the community. Regardless of the process selected, it must begin with a care for the spiritual well-being of people. This begins with the question the church must answer, "What is a person worth to you?"[53] Until this question is answered, and the church comes to grips with its true focus, no real community outreach or development can be performed.

Jesus had a heart for the people, and the church must have the same heart if it hopes to achieve anything approaching Jesus's command. Jesus ministered to a population of roughly three million people, "teaching, preaching the Gospel, and healing every kind of disease and sickness."[54] Their needs touched him, and he sought to provide for them. This is clear in the book of Matthew, "Seeing the people, He felt compassion for them" (Matt 9:36). Jesus saw their spiritual condition and was moved with compassion. The individual meant everything to Jesus. The church must follow suit and have compassion for the community. This compassion must address the community's spiritual needs and seek to develop mature Christians who will seek God in every aspect of their lives. By default, their disposition will improve in every area of life.

The idea the church will seek spiritual development of the community is a given, so the other area the church needs to consider is where and what other needs they are willing and able to address within the community. In the modern era, the church also "needs to

---

[53.] Neil Cole, *Organic Church*, 143.
[54.] Ibid., 145.

continue to exercise power and self-determination in ecclesiastical and civil affairs as a requirement and in defense of the virtues of black manhood and womanhood in American society."[55] This decision should be based on their sincere desire to engage with their compassion for the people. This requires accomplishment of a self-audit, seeking to determine the missional capabilities of the church and its desire and willingness to address other needs in the community. This self-audit among many things will show the need for strong, spirit-filled leadership.

Leadership

The first necessity in the church's pursuit to engage the community is the establishment of a single source of leadership. A leader sets the example, creates the environment, decides the approach, prioritizes the effort, ensures the appropriate focus is maintained and desired effect achieved.

Biblical leadership mandates the model for this position and only takes place when divinely appointed men and women respond in obedience to God's call.[56] This appointment also ensures that leaders follow a model that resembles servants and stewards, not dictators and monarchs. Leaders must realize they cannot solve every problem, and they cannot solve any problem alone. This attitude should be built on a humility that leads to self-discipline and keeps them "committed and focused over the long haul even when tempted by personal gain or by the inevitable distraction of personal pleasure."[57]

Aspects of leadership that are traditionally not considered are mental and emotional dynamics. It's about who you are, deep down, that impacts your relationship with God, with others, with yourself,

---

[55]. James C. Cavendish, "Church-Based Community Activism: A Comparison of Black and White Catholic Congregations," *Journal for the Scientific Study of Religion* 39, no. 3 (2000), 64.

[56]. James D. Berkley, *Leadership Handbook of Management & Administration* (Grand Rapids, MI: Baker Books, 2007), 147.

[57]. Ibid., 62.

and the whole created order."[58] The mental aspect in leadership is important to the longevity of the leader. The stability comes from the leader's ability to stand strong and remain consistent during stressful and nonstressful times. This combination of emotional and mental stability is a defining factor in the success of the leader and ministry team.

Ministry Team Selection

After the leader is in position, the church is ready to identify its team that will do the work of outreach and community development. The church considers volunteers to be a part of this outreach. They must determine what type of volunteer is required, what the volunteers will be expected to do, what resources are available to be used by the volunteers, and what training, if any, the volunteers require.[59]

The volunteer ministry team will be composed of members of the church pursuing community development and thus should be known by the church and leadership team.

However, because of the type of volunteer work the team will perform, the church should consider a screening process, requiring volunteers to sign a volunteer agreement and provide training.[60] To ensure organization and clear responsibility, each volunteer should be provided with specific instructions on their role and expected duties.

---

[58] "Real Ministry in a Complex World. Emotional Stability; an Interview with Peter Scazzero" *Leadership Journal,* (2012): 2–4, accessed June 23, 2017.

[59] U.S. Department of Health and Human Services, "Successful Strategies for Recruiting, Training, and Utilizing Volunteers: A Guide for Faith- and Community-Based Service Providers," *Substance Abuse and Mental Health Services Administration Faith-Based and Community Initiative,* 1–4, accessed December 7, 2016, https://www.samhsa.gov/sites/default/files/volunteer_handbook.pdf.

[60] "Successful Strategies," A-5.

Church Capability Assessment

Once a leader is identified, the volunteer team is in place, the church can identify where it will engage, how it will engage, how often it will engage, and the resources it has available to sponsor this engagement. This self-audit ensures that the church remains true to its abilities and capabilities and does not go beyond identified fiscal limits. This assessment will ensure that the church gains a handle on its resources so that it protects itself, especially in a demoralized society.[61]

The assessment provides the necessary insight for the churches in order for it to maintain and sustain itself. Three critical areas must be assessed: how the church relates, what the church values, and how the church defines itself.[62]

Assessing Community Needs

After the church is sure it has a grasp on its abilities, capabilities, and God-ordained mission, it must begin to assess how these capabilities can be best applied to affect the needs of the community. At a minimum, the church must become knowledgeable of the community's beliefs, history, people, politics, and institutions.[63] As the church tries to determine the needs of the community, it must realize there are many categories of need that must be considered. Among these are belonging, self-esteem, and security.[64]

While keeping the above categories in mind, the church must determine how it can best "affirm the dignity of people, motivate

---

[61.] Walter Rauschenbusch, *Christianity and the Social Crisis in the 21stt Century* (New York, NY: harper One, 2007), 235.

[62.] Michael Todd Wilson and Brad Hoffman, *Preventing Ministry Failure* (Downers Grove, IL.: Intervarsity Press, 2007), 26.

[63.] Ray Blake and Jim Hart, *The Urban Christian: Effective Ministry in Today's Urban World* (Downers Grove, IL.: InterVarsity Press, 1987), 109.

[64.] Avneet Kaur, "Maslow's Need Hierarchy Theory: Allocations and Criticisms," *Global Journal of Management and Business* 3. No. 10 (2013): pp. 1061–1064.

them, and help them take responsibility for their own lives."[65] In this pursuit, the church must consider disorder in the lives of those they are trying to reach that may be the result of meaningless living.[66] To reorder lives, the church must help the individual find meaning in their lives.

Areas of Engagement

The church is now ready to determine what areas, in addition to extended salvation, it will engage to assist in community improvement and development. Using the needs of the focus area and the resources available in the church and government support, the church will seek to influence the community by seeking improvements in a myriad of areas where feasible government assistance can be helpful in sustaining the initiatives.[67]

In the midst of the prior-mentioned initiatives, it is critically important that children be given primacy. For example, in the United States, there are 415,129 children in foster care. Of this group, 24 percent are African American. The percentages by race and ethnic group are astonishing.[68] Specifically, Alabama had 3,243 children in foster care in 2014.[69]

---

[65] Perkins, 198.

[66] Richard A. Swenson, Margin: *Restoring Emotional, Physical, Financial, and Time Reserves to Overloaded Lives* (Colorado Springs, CO: NavPress, 2004), 15.

[67] Adam S. Weinberg, *Urban Recycling and the Search for Sustainable Community Development* (Princeton, N.J.: Princeton University Press, 2000), 36.

[68] US Department of Health and Human Services, Administration for Children and Families, "Administration on Children, Youth and Families, Children's Bureau. The AFCARS Report," accessed December 13, 2016, https://www.acf.hhs.gov/sites/default/files/cb/afcarsreport22.pdf.

[69] US Department of Health and Human Services, Administration for Children and Families, Administration on Children, Youth and Families, Children's Bureau, "Numbers of Children Entering Foster Care by State FY 2005-FY 2014," accessed December 13, 2016, https://acf.hhs.gov/programs/cb.

An additional statistic, for example, in North Alabama alone, 59,000 children are considered food insecure.[70] These are children who do not have access to or skip at least one meal each day. This need to skip meals can be attributed to the high poverty rate in the state. Alabama has one of the highest poverty rates in the country, coming in at 19 percent.[71]

The elderly is another group that the church should prioritize in its community outreach and development activities. As of July 2015, 15.7 percent of Alabama residents were over sixty-five years old.[72] Additionally, 39 percent of homes in Alabama contain an elderly member or a member with disabilities.[73]

Community Support Programs

One of the greatest mistakes that a church can make in its efforts to reach out to and provide support for the community it is serving is to assume that it must do all of its outreach on its own. In effect, where feasible, the church must collaborate with locally based organizations as well as federal and state organizations.

Although there is minimal evidence, available information shows that effective collaboration between the church and social based entities can produce effective results.

When addressing outreach in terms of racial composition, isolated ethnographic accounts and small-scale studies have documented church-sponsored programs and community economic development initiatives aimed at developing collaborative alliances. For example, Eng and Hatch (1991) developed one of the most

---

[70.] Kathryn Strickland, "Beyond Charity to Systematic Food System Change." North Alabama Food Bank. Child Food Insecurity Training Briefing. (2013).

[71.] Alemayehu Bishaw, "2010 Census. Poverty: 2019-2011," *American Community Survey Briefs* (Issued September 2012): 11-01, accessed December 13, 2016. https://www.census.gov/prod/2012pubs/acsbr11-01.pdf.

[72.] . Ibid.

[73.] Center on Budget and Policy Priorities, "Fact Sheet: Alabama Federal Rental Assistance," (March 30, 2017): accessed December 13, 2016. http://www.cbpp.org/sites/default/files/atoms/files/4-13-11hous-AL.pdf

notable church-sponsored programs, collaborating with area service agencies to use rural churches in North Carolina as a focus for health promotion activities. This and other variations of community-based partnerships recognize that religious institutions occupy a position of trust and respect in Black communities.[74]

The significance of the church's engagement with social services programs is centered on the position of the church in the community. "Since the church is a potential resource for bridging the gap between state, federal, and local agencies and the informal services provisions, collaboration between agencies and religious organizations can offer new opportunities to meet the needs of parishioners and community members."[75]

First and foremost, the church must be aware of its responsibility, the history of this responsibility and, more importantly, the biblical mandate associated with community outreach and engagement. The church is in somewhat of a crisis, not a crisis of survival but a crisis of "rediscovering its purpose."[76] The first step in this recovery is uncovering its purpose. The main goal of the church is reaching the lost for Christ. A subcategory of this purpose is the responsibility to improve the lives and develop the members of the community. Although spiritual, a relationship with Christ will affect the entire being of an individual. To this end, the church must realize that the community is in a crisis. Furthermore, it must understand that whether it is the crisis of the church or that of the community, "crisis events are a part of life originating from God's specific direction, from the natural progression of creation, or from humanity's spiritual deprivation."[77]

[74.] Alex D. Colvin and Darron D. Garner, "Social Work and the African American Church: Using a Collaborative Approach to Address Service Delivery," North American Association of Christians in Social Work; A Vital Presence in Social Work, accessed December 5, 2016. http://www.nacsw.org/Publications/Proceedings2010/ColvinASocialWork.pdf.

[75.] Ibid.

[76.] James W. Thompson, *Church According to Paul: Rediscovering the Community Conformed to Christ* (Grand Rapids, US: Baker Academic, 2014), ii, accessed May 1, 2017, ProQuest ebrary.

[77.] Timothy Clinton and George Ohlschlager, *Competent Christian Counseling: Foundations & Practice of Compassionate Soul Care* (Colorado Springs, CO:

This in no way relieves the government or other entities from the legal responsibilities of caring for taxpayers. This is evident in government support programs like food stamps, housing assistance, Medicare, and Medicaid which are necessary but not the final solutions. Ultimately, divine intervention can't be ignored as the glue which holds the church and all of humanity together.

Conclusion

The community, especially the Black community, whether in the immediate vicinity of the church or farther out, should be the focus of church engagement and development. The church has the biblical mandate to reach out into the community in order to effect the spiritual well-being and lives of residents. The church is the beneficiary of community member attendance and support. These very members pour their hearts into their ministries and, in turn, fill church coffers with their limited funds. It is the church with the heart of God, the mind of Christ, and the power of Christ within that should be the overall driver of all initiatives. The member participation, the mission and purpose of the church requires the church to pursue ministries to enhance the life of church and community members.

WaterBrook Press, 2002), 602.

Spirituality: Oft the Missing Link in African American Mental Health

Dr. Creigs C. Beverly

*This article describes the importance of the spiritual domain
in the treatment of African Americans in mental health
systems and offers a set of practice questions which begin to
unleash the therapeutic potential pertaining thereto.*

It is not uncommon in American culture to hear references to the totality of human existence framed within the trilinear paradigm: mind, body, and soul. Soul is often exchanged for or becomes interchangeable with the spirit. Therefore, mind, body and soul as a singular construct is equivalent to, and synonymous with, mind, body, and spirit.

The axiom in the field of mental health is that individuals who effectively integrate each of these components into the formation of personality have the requisite foundation for successful social functioning and "good mental health."

Caution, however, is advised in any discussion of successful social functioning and/or "good mental health." This is important because human feelings and behavior are extremely variable (Mechanic 1989). What may be considered abnormal behavior in one social or cultural context, may well be considered normal in another. As a consequence, in trying to describe the characteristics of people with positive mental health, some clinicians and investigators have sought to define various persistent aspects of social character or personality that could be viewed independently of the social context (Mechanic 1989). Instead they emphasize such themes as social sensitivity, the capacity for environmental mastery, a unifying outlook on life, self-actualization, and self-acceptance (Mechanic 1989, Jahoda 1958).

Regardless of the dialogue and debate around what in fact constitutes positive mental health within the general mental health field, the literature is replete with information on the relationship between mind and body in the formation of personality and positive mental health.

Why has spirituality received so little attention in mental health literature and even less in the treatment of African-Americans who are recipients of mental health services? Several points of departure are applicable in order to answer this question, but a lesson from Ghana, West Africa, appears to be particularly instructive.

There is a concept in Ghana, West Africa, which states "We must learn to see the music and hear the dance." Inherent in this statement is a reversal of what is perceived to be the logical sequence, i.e., hearing the music and seeing the dance. The explanation given by village elders is that if one is only able to comprehend the obvious, then the lessons to be learned from the not so obvious get lost in translation.

The relationship between this West African lesson and spirituality is that spirituality cannot be understood or appreciated if we don't have the courage to explore a domain of life which cannot be found on the chart of chemical elements which does not adhere to universal laws of physics; which cannot be touched, or smelled as would be the case with organic matter; and which cannot be reduced into a mathematical formula or subjected to the rigors of DNA analyses. In other words, if spirituality can't be understood within the ground rules of scientific inquiry, then it either doesn't exist as a factor or is of no consequence. Sermabeikian (1994) states that:

> To understand the spiritual perspective, we must
> be willing to reverse our usual way of thinking and
> looking, which is linear and externally focused.

We must look beyond what is easily counted and accounted for and examine what does not fit into our categories and conceptions of the world. There can be no preconceived notions about what may be helpful. The spiritual perspective requires that we look beyond the fears and limitations of the immediate problem with the goal of discovering something inspirational and meaningful rather than focusing on the past and on pathology.

In a similar view, Cowley (1993) discusses the spiritual domain of life within the context of transpersonal theory and asserts that:

Social workers in the post-modem age are being challenged by individual and societal problems that are lodged in the spiritual dimension. For many, these challenges require that they become knowledgeable about a relatively unfamiliar theoretical approach based in transpersonal psychology and primarily concerned with disturbances of the psyche or soul. The distinctive focus of transpersonal psychology is its emphasis on spiritual growth and the transformation of consciousness. Prime concerns of transpersonal theory are the search for ultimate values, peak or mystical experiences, and unitive consciousness and the legitimization of spiritual practice. Transpersonal theory has developed in response to a search for meaning that goes beyond existential levels and seeks to incorporate higher states of consciousness and spiritual connection.

Both Cowley and Sermabeikian acknowledge previous attempts by other authors to overcome Western ideological bias and truly address the third leg of the human trilogy: mind, body, and spirit (emphasis on spirit). Most notably among these are Jung (1959), Maslow (1962) and Wilber and Brown (1986).

Dorr (1984) states that our spirituality is revealed not so much by the theories we propose as by the way we act and react. It is an implicit theology which, if we are reflective and articulate, may eventually become explicit, and then it is very convincing because it represents a truth that is lived.

The under representation, understanding and use of spirituality in the mental health field is a life limiting factor for all human beings. For people of African descent, whose history is steeped in spirituality, it is not only a life limiting factor but also a life denying factor.

Spirituality Defined

In a generic sense, spirituality is an idiomatic construct which provides for its holder, both individually and collectively, a sense of connectedness between self and the universe; between personal power and all power; between knowing and believing; between harmony and dissonance; between the explained and the inexplicable; between the tangible and the intangible; and between worldly trauma and ultimate peace.

It is important to distinguish here between spirituality and religion. The two are incorrectly used interchangeably. Religion is an organized or institutionalized set of attitudes, beliefs, and practices. These attitudes, beliefs and practices vary depending upon the particular denomination with which one is affiliated. Religion is deeply steeped in dogma or doctrine and it is not unusual for one church authority to proclaim that the particular doctrines which undergird its practices and procedures are the only legitimate ones and all others are some aberration thereof.

Spirituality doesn't require denominational affiliation, nor is it restricted by doctrine. It is universal and at the very same time idiomatic and peculiar to the individual. Therefore, an individual can be spiritual without belonging to a church or a particular religious denomination. This is not to suggest by any means that one cannot be religious and also spiritual.

In a general sense, spirituality can best be understood in the inexplicable knowledge that a mother knows her child is in trouble without being told. It is the ability of a person to get quiet enough and still enough to get in touch with the genuineness within oneself. It is the ability to listen to the silence of one's own soul, knowing it is the loudest sound one will ever hear.

It is when you say nothing, but you have said everything. It is the symmetry which comes from discovering one's personal gifts and finding the appropriate medium for their human expression. It is in the final analysis the peace which results from making peace with oneself: seeing the music and hearing the dance.

Spirituality and African-American Mental Health

African-American mental health represents the confluence of mind, body and spirit (soul) such that the human organism and/or the broader collective thereof, is able to navigate (direction); orchestrate (organize/mobilize); and negotiate (successfully transact and interact) social reality in ways and means consistent with maximizing creative human potential, without deliberate violence or violation of the rights of others to achieve same.

Central to this definition of African-American mental health is personal justice, defined as fairness in one's interpersonal relationships and systemic justice, defined as fairness in institutional interfaces, i.e. when societal inconsistencies give way to a goodness of fit between words and deeds.

The strength of African-American spirituality and its central applicability in mental health treatment and prevention services can't be understood in the absence of a historical backdrop. This is the only way to understand how people of African descent, subjects of one of the most brutal and inhumane systems known to man—slavery—have been able to sustain themselves in the midst of unabating assaultive environments. No one has done a more superb job of framing these beginnings than has Vincent Harding (1981) in his seminal piece, *There is a River: The Struggle for Freedom in America*:

> It began at the edge of our homeland, where the verdant forests and tropical bush gave way gradually to the sandy stretches of the Guinea Coast. It began at the mouth of the rivers, from that northern point where the Senegal and Gambia pour their troubled streams into the waters around Cape Verde, down the thousands of miles of coastline to the place where the mighty river Conga breaks out into the ocean. On these shores near the mouths of these rivers, we first saw the ships.
>
> There was no way to know it then, but their crews of men and boys came from many ports and many pasts to find the shores of. Africa. They sailed from Amsterdam and Lisbon, from Nantes and La Rochelle, from Bristol and London. From Newport and Boston on ships with strange names. They came to us on <u>Brotherhood</u> and <u>John the Baptist</u>, on <u>Justice</u> and <u>Integrity</u>, on <u>Gift of God and Liberty</u>; they came on the good ship <u>Jesus</u>. But by the time our weary lines of chained and mourning travelers saw vessels riding on the coastal waves, there could be but one name, one meaning, captivity. Thus, it was on the edges of our continent where some of us gulped down handfuls of sand in a last effort to hold the reality of the land—that the long struggle for black freedom began.

Since the arrival of the first African slaves in Jamestown, Virginia, nearly four hundred years ago, black people have had to survive in environments hostile to their presence and in many ways committed to their destruction.

History is replete with lynchings, beatings, rape, political and economic disenfranchisement, discrimination of every variety, social marginality, and invisibility.

Even after years of struggle, civil rights laws, affirmative action and other compensatory justice measures, people of African descent continue to experience an imperfect freedom. Much of the current day mayhem and destruction reflects a displacement of internal rage Onto each other. This displacement has resulted in black on black homicides becoming the leading cause of death among young black men between the ages of 17 and 24. Drugs, savage inequality in the educational system, federal disinvestment, and lack of viable jobs in cities are also major contributing factors to continued marginal status among far too many people of African descent.

Given these unrelenting assaults upon the human dignity of people of African descent, both internal and external, a persistent question remains: How is it possible to maintain sanity as a member of a population cohort constantly under siege and assault? The implication is that any group which has experienced the levels of unabated abuse people of African-American descent have and continue to experience, should at worst be extinct and at best insane. There is, arguably, only one explanation of why black people are neither extinct, nor all crazy: black spirituality.

One of the leading African-American thinkers on the concept of black spirituality is Dr. Wade Nobles, Clinical Psychologist on the faculty of San Francisco University. In a recent two-hour presentation at the University of Michigan entitled: "African Psychologic Illumination of the Spirit," Dr. Nobles argued that all black people need to know is already inside each black person and that, as a people, we need to stop listening to Western psychology types who give us crazy-named disorders they would have us believe are the problem. "We've got to get back to the spirit." He referenced "Sakhu," an African word meaning spirit and is a practice dating back to the 15th century. It covers a set of religious and psychological teachings that focus on meditation and the importance of the spirit in having a healthy mind and body.

Black Spirituality—Defense and Offense

Leonard E. Barrett (1974) equates the concept of black spirituality with what he terms soul-force:

> Soul force in "Black-Talk" describes that quality of life that has enabled Black people to survive the horrors of their "diaspora." The experience of slavery, and its later repercussions still remain to be dealt with; and "soul" signifies the moral and emotional fiber of the black man that enables him to see his dilemmas clearly and at the same time encourages and sustains him in his struggles. "Force" connotes strength, power, intense effort and a will to live. The combined words—"Soul-Force"—describe the racial inheritance of the new world African; it is that which characterizes his life-style, his world view and his endurance under conflict. It is his frame of reference vis-à-vis the wider world and his blueprint for the struggle from bondage to freedom. Soul-force is that power of the black man which turns sorrow into joy, crying into laughter, and defeat into victory. It is patience while suffering, determination while frustrated and hope while in despair. It derives its impetus from the ancestral heritage of Africa, its refinement from the bondage of slavery, and its continuing vitality from the conflict of the present. It expresses itself collectively as well as through charismatic leaders. In addition, it can express itself in states of acquiescence, avoidance and separation. So there

is no end to the permutations and combinations
of the restless "soul." Soul is visceral rather than
intellectual, irrational rather than rational; it is
art rather than logic.

Black spirituality can be heard in the mourns of black mothers
who keep their families together under tremendous odds; it can be
heard among church elders who lead prayer meetings without ever
speaking a word; it can be heard in freedom songs, e.g., "We Shall
Overcome"; it can be seen in the empty place settings on dinner
tables in black homes; it can be seen when brothers on street corners
pour the first drink of wine to the ground in recognition of those no
longer here; it can be seen in the pouring of libations to the ances-
tors; it can be heard in the unifying chant, harambee; and it can be
seen in the wrinkled faces of old black men whose lives have been the
epitome of "Nobody Knows the Trouble I've Seen."

It is evidenced by black sharecroppers who educated their children on subsistence wages. It is evidenced in the collective pennies
of our forefathers who built <u>Benedict College</u> in South Carolina;
<u>Shaw College</u> in Virginia; <u>Bishop College</u> in Texas; <u>Leland College</u> in
Louisiana; <u>Selma University</u> in Alabama; <u>Florida Memorial College</u>
in Florida; <u>Roger Williams College</u> in Tennessee; <u>Simmons College</u>
in Kentucky; <u>Arkansas Baptist</u> in Arkansas; <u>Storer College</u> in West
Virginia and many others.

It was evidenced during the darkest hours of the civil rights
movement, when it appeared as if all hope was lost and somehow the
old and the young, the educated and the illiterate, the doctors and
the cotton picker, found the strength to keep on struggling. It was
the force that compelled Fannie Lou Hamer to say that she was tired
of being tired, but she would never get too tired to keep on fighting
for black freedom.

Black spirituality gives you the strength to have hope in the
midst of despair; to be confident in the face of doubt; to stand firm
in the whirlwind of controversy; to see possibilities when all options
appear to be exhausted; and to believe in the absence of any empirical
evidence to support your beliefs.

It is singing and sharing; dancing and fighting; shouting and serving; making love and making up; believing and building; rocking in ecstasy and resisting evil; teaching and politicizing; preaching and socializing; saving souls and strengthening schools; building and developing; uniting and unifying; being and becoming; it is the force within all black people that says you will not destroy my humanity, regardless of what you do. (Bennett 1992)

Perhaps Madhubuti (1990) understood best the meaning of black spirituality when he framed his "S" curve of African-American Life:

Source	Soil	Seeing
Soul	Self	Spirit
Strength	Structure	Searching
Security	Study	Student
Serious	Space	Stop-Time
Smile	Simplicity	Silence
Stillness	Solitude	Sharing
Saving	Service	Specialness
Support	Subtle	Stimulate
Struggle	Shining	Saneness
Speaking	Skepticism	Substance
Success	Steady	and Ready for Sisters

Black spirituality is defensive because it serves as a rebuttal to the world's offensive behaviors toward people of color. It is offensive because it serves as a proactive framework which allows black people to see beyond the contingencies of today and envision a time and a place of transcendence and unfettered human development. It is indeed the ability to see the music and hear the dance. It is invisible as a force, but visible in products of black life, past, present, and future!

Spirituality and Practice

One of the most widely used diagnostic tools within the mental health field is the "psychosocial assessment." In many respects, it is a biographical history of clients designed to ascertain, over the life span, an assessment of development phases and the mastery or incompleteness of them. The assumption is that difficulty in successful social functioning can be traced to some previous unresolved or incomplete developmental phase. These phases are usually divided into childhood, pre-adolescence, adolescence, young adulthood, middle age, and old age. A plethora of books and scholarly articles have been written on the meaning and significance of life cycle development. Among these, several are particularly instructive (Hall and Lindzey 1978, Lidz 1976, White and Parkam 1990, Sheehy 1977).

A cursory review of these assessments in the mental health field would reveal almost no attention to spirituality as a meaningful and significant component in human development, not to mention a major factor in social dysfunction. It is acknowledged that this gross oversight is important for all human beings, but it is especially important when working with African-Americans receiving services from various mental health systems.

Any psychosocial assessment of African-Americans must be extended to include the spiritual domain. This is absolutely critical because the African world view begins with a holistic conception of the human condition. As expressed by White and Parkam (1990):

> There appears to be a definite correspondence between the African ethos and the Afro-American world view in terms of the focus on emotional vitality, interdependence, collective survival, the oral tradition, perception of time, harmonious

blending, and the role of the elderly. Some have questioned the utility of an African normative base, given the enormous tribal and geographical variability among African people. However, to discount the presence of an African norm because of differences is analogous to missing the forest for the trees. Certainly, there are individual differences, but there are more commonalities than difference, and those common themes provide the foundation for the African world view.

The African world view begins with a holistic conception of the human condition. There is no mind-body or affective-cognitive dualism. The human organism is conceived as a totality made up of a series of interlocking systems. This total person is simultaneously a feeling, experiencing, sensualizing, sensing, and knowing human being living in a dynamic, vitalistic world where everything is interrelated and endowed with the supreme force of life. There is a sense of aliveness, intensity, and animation in the music, dance, song, language, and lifestyles of Africans. Emotions are not labeled as bad; therefore, there is no need to repress feelings of compassion, love, joy, or sensuality.

The essential understanding to be gleaned from White and Parkam is that people of African descent view the world as a set of interlocking systems and that who they were; who they are; and who they become is a function of the confluence and interplay of all these systems. In effect cosmology and ontology are just as relevant to people of African descent as are biology and genetics to people in general.

In clinical practice, the primary diagnostic question is: Is the patient's problem physical or mental? (Levy 1994). Here it becomes clear where traditional clinical focus is concentrated: disorders are either viewed as physical biological/ neurochemical/physiological/organic) or mental (psychological/psychogenic/ functional). Nowhere does spiritual surface as even a consideration in personal disorders. For people of African descent, what ails them is neither singularly physical, mental or spiritual, rather it is the confluence of all three.

We do a fine job with questions in the physical and mental domains, but we must also become comfortable with questions in the spiritual domain, the answers to which may not fit easily into DSM IV criteria. (The diagnostic and statistical manual (Bible) in the mental health field).

Examples of the types of questions relevant for African-American clients which enfranchise spirituality as a salient component in understanding the context and content of their presenting problems would be: What do you do when there isn't anything else to do? Can you tell me at what time in your life were you at the greatest peace with yourself? Given everything that has happened to you, how do you find the strength to keep going? What does it mean to you to be authentic and can you give me an example of your authenticity? What does it mean to be a whole person, i.e., what does it take to be a whole person? When you are deeply troubled by something, are there particular songs you think about or sing? Can you give me an example of a song you might think of or sing when you are deeply troubled? How are you able to find beauty in an ugly world? What are your special and unique gifts? What is your purpose and mission in life—why has the creator of the universe blessed the world with your presence?

The answer to these questions and others similarly structured can assist the practitioner in resolving the false trichotomy between mind, body, and spirit and lead to the ultimate understanding that one, plus one, plus one, equals one and not three. Figure 1 illustrates the integration of all three domains.

Figure 1: Integration of the Human Trilogy:
Mind, Body and Spirit (Soul)

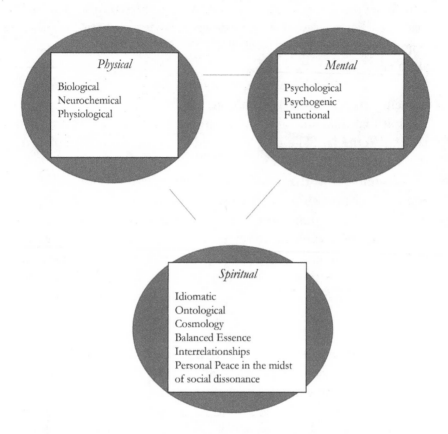

For people of African descent, health is neither a function singularly of the physical domain, mental domain or the spiritual domain. It is a function of all three simultaneously. There is no physical without a mental, nor a mental without a spiritual and the converse, however paired is equally true.

In an advanced course in Social Policy and Mental Health, being conducted at Wayne State University in Detroit, Michigan, an

African-American female student, in a reaction paper to a class discussion on the role of spirituality in mental health treatment wrote:

> The discussion to being open to investigating the spiritual as well the mental and physical aspects of individuals in regards to psychopathology, made me reflect on my own meaning of the word spiritual.
>
> As a child I was exposed to the spiritual faith by my maternal grandfather who was a spiritualist minister for over fifty years. I learned from my grandfather what spiritualism is and does. In brief, spiritualism teaches personal responsibility, it removes all fears of death—which is really the portal of the spirit world, it teaches not that man has a soul but that man is a soul and has a body.
>
> Furthermore, man is a spiritual being now, even while encased in flesh.
>
> And those who have passed are conscious— not asleep. Spiritualism brings to the surface man's spiritual gifts such as inspiration, clairvoyance, clairaudience and healing powers, it teaches that the spark of divinity dwells in all and as a flower gradually unfolds and develops in the spirit spheres, spiritualism is God's message to mortals—declaring that there is no death.
>
> In the spirit world, man retains his individuality and the unfoldment of his mental, oral and spiritual faculties is continued not unlike those pertaining to this world. Spiritualism is the broad educator, the great redeemer, the emancipator which releases human souls from the bondage of superstition and ignorance. Spiritualism has given freedom to slaves and broken shackles of mental bondage.

It has been somewhat frightening for me to realize that since I have been working in the mental health field, my assessment of individuals has narrowed to only recognizing the physical and mental aspects. If by chance circumstances were different and someone had to assess me, I certainly wouldn't want anyone to discount the spiritual part of my being. I realize now that I have to shift my own paradigm to include the spiritual for other people.

The most instructive sentence in this student's discussion is "If by chance circumstances were different and someone had to assess me, I certainly wouldn't want anyone to discount the spiritual part of my being." For this student, it is clear that to discount a part of who she is, is in essence to discount her as a person.

Figure 2 represents a summary pictorial of the role spirituality plays in African-American mental health. It begins with the objective reality of African-American life in American society. For people of African descent, personal devaluation, social injustice, societal inconsistency and personal impotence (Chestang 1972) represent their objective reality. The internalization of this objective reality, that is their subjective interpretation of it, leads to black rage (Grier and Cobbs 1980).

This rage, depending upon how it is processed, can lead to insanity and severe states of personal dysfunction or to a transcendent state of mental health. The key determinant is the filter through which the rage is processed. When this rage is filtered through an African-American spiritual funnel, the probable outcome is positive mental health. If, however, this rage is not filtered through an African-American spiritual funnel, the probability is mental illness or other self-defeating behaviors. The inability of African-Americans to filter their rage through a spiritual funnel is a consequence of the underdevelopment of one's spiritual domain of existence. The spiritual domain is present in all people of African descent, but like all other aspects of life and living, it has to be recognized, nurtured, and developed.

As long as African-Americans seek to define their personhood, worthiness and validation in the context of Eurocentric paradigms, mental illness and social dysfunction are inevitable. Their presence in mental health treatment systems can very often be located at the confluence of trying to be "somebody" in a world which constantly devalues them and reinforces their nobodiness. Those who have well developed spiritual domains escape this painful dilemma because they don't seek validation from an invalidating society. They have learned that it is difficult, if not impossible to fight an enemy who has outposts in your mind.

Fundamental to treating African-Americans in mental health systems is to assist them in rediscovering their spiritual domain. In effect, assisting them in recalling that which they already know.

Figure 2: The Role of Spirituality in African American
Mental health: An Analytical Paradigm

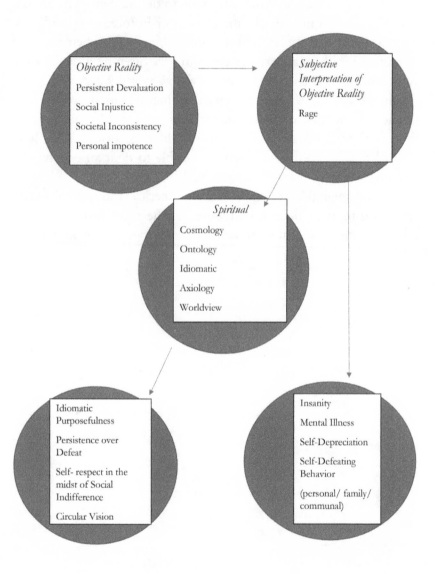

Developed by Dr. Creigs Beverly, Wayne State University, 1995

REFERENCES

Barrett, Leonard E. 1974. *Soul-Force African Heritage in Afro-American Religion*. New York: Anchor Press/Doubleday 1–2.

Bennet, Lerone. 1992. *The Challenge of Blackness*. Chicago: Johnson Publishing Co. Inc.

Chestang, Leon W. 1972. "Character Development in a Hostile Society." Occasional Paper No. #3, Chicago, Illinois University of Chicago.

Cowley, Au. Deane S. 1993. "Transpersonal Social Work: A Theory for the 1990s." *Social Work*, 8(2). 527.

Dorr, Donal. 1984. *Spirituality and Justice*. New York: Orbis Books 8–18.

Grier, William H. and Price M. Cobbs. 1980. *Black Rage*. New York: Basic Books Inc.

Hall, Calvin and Gardner Lindsey. 1978. *Theories of Personality*. New York: John Wiley & Sons.

Harding, Vincent. 1981. *There Is a River: The Black Struggle for Freedom in America*. New York: Harcourt Brace Jovanovich, Publishers, pp 3–4.

Jahoda, Marie. 1958. *Current Concepts of Positive Mental Health*. New York: Basic Books.

Jung, C. G. 1959. *The Archetypes and the Collective Unconscious*. Princeton, NJ: Princeton University Press.

Lidz, Theodore. 1976. *The Person: His and Her Development Throughout the Life Cycle*. New York: Basic Books.

Madhubuti, Haki R. 1990. *Black Men, Obsolete, Single, Dangerous*. Chicago: Third World Press. 215–219.

Maslow, A. H. 1962. *Toward a Psychology of Being*. Princeton, NJ: Van Nostrand Press.

Mechanic, David. 1989. *Mental Health and Social Policy*. New Jersey: Prentice Hall, pp 1–3.

Nobel, Wade. 1994. "African Psychologic Illumination of the Spirit." Special Seminar, University of Michigan at Ann Arbor Clinical Psychology Department.

Sermabeikian, Patricia. 1994. "Our Clients, Ourselves: The Spiritual Perspective and Social Work Practice." *Social Work*, 39 (2), p. 179.

Sheehy, Gail. 1977. *Passages: Predictable Crises of Adult Life*. New York: Bantam Books.

White, Joseph and Thomas Parkham. 1990. *The Psychology of Blacks: An African American Perspective*. New Jersey: Prentice Hall.

Zastrow, Charles and Karen K. Ashman. 1987. *Understanding Human Behavior and the Social Environment*. Chicago: Nelson-Hall Publishers.

Afterword
Can the Black Church
Survive This?

Rev. Ernest L. Williams

The year 2020 will go down in history as a year of strange occurrences. The year began in the backdrop of an impeachment trial of the president of the United States. As the year took off, the world was plagued with the coronavirus that took full swing in March of 2020. On May 25, George Floyd, an unarmed Black man was killed by police in Minneapolis, Minnesota, over an alleged forged twenty-dollar bill. This incident, along with so many other cases of police brutality, seemed to have been the breaking point of racial injustices against African Americans. Protest demonstrations, marches, vandalism, and arsenic activity throughout the county took center stage as Black, (mostly) White, and other ethnic groups united in one effort to say to America, "Black Lives Matter." With the deaths of so many due to the coronavirus, the United States and the world have been at a standstill socially and economically.

Amid all of this, churches across this country have been forced to close their doors to the public due to COVID-19 concerns. Churches have had to resort to broadcasting their services online or resort to innovative methods of social-distance-guided services such as drive-up or parking-lot services. Many churches have found this mode of worship difficult, especially for the elderly and technologically challenged church members. This new "normal" for worship is also affecting the financial stability of churches. With church members not present at church buildings and some members with reservations about online giving, churches are finding this new change financially burdensome. Who suffers the most in this pandemic? Small businesses and Black churches suffer the most. Thus, I raise what I believe to be an appropriate question, Can the Black church survive this? "This" refers to the current downward trend in society that is causing the church to be irrelevant socially, economically, and spiritually. I believe the Black church can survive the current crisis if it adheres to the following: adaptive measures, making the right investments, and not losing focus on the mission of the church.

Can the Black Church Survive This? Adaptability

If the Black church in America is to have a voice at the national table, the Black church must learn to adapt to the growing and changing times within which it exists. The Black church is the least in terms of technology. Our larger Black churches have overcome this hurdle. But for the vast majority of Black churches, technology has been a taboo. Why is there a fear of adapting to technology in the Black church? For the most part, Black churches are either run by elderly members, or the leadership is sensitive to the disadvantages of the elderly membership. As a result, younger Blacks are joining larger churches where technology is the norm. How to overcome this disparity? Black churches must have as a part of their leadership people who are familiar with technology and who are willing to implement technology in the church. Interestingly, most churches have members who are currently employed on jobs that utilize some form of information technology (IT). Churches will be amazed by the amount of wealth of knowledge and experience within congregations.

The greatest fear is for the elderly leadership to give up (relinquish) its authority to a younger and more technologically savvy congregant. However, if the Black church is to have a footing in its future, the change must happen now. Barnabas recognized this shift in culture and in leadership and relinquished his authority over to a younger and probably more trained person by the name of Paul (Acts 9:27, 11:25–26).

Can the Black Church Survive This? Investments
Rev. Ernest L. Williams

The next phase of the Black church's survival is its ability, or its inability for that matter, to invest. Historic trends show that African Americans and the Black church are more inclined to contribute to "religious" charitable organizations versus other nonprofits.[78] The giving power of the Black church was comparable to their White counterparts. This implies that African Americans are less likely to invest in any other entity other than the church. The Blackbaud report of 2015 shows 70 percent of Caucasians contributing to charitable organizations, with only 12 percent of African American contributions.

The Black church can be a leader in investing in its own future. To do this, the Black church must raise investments to the forefront. Investments involve three forces: fear, faith, and the future. Those who do not invest probably do not due to fear. With respect to investments, fear has been the crippling agent in the Black church. The Black church is comfortable maintaining its current status. But its current status is a status of isolation. The church finds itself isolated from the very people that Christ has called it to serve. Investment involves being optimistic about the future. This is not blind optimism. This future optimism is centered on biblical principles. The first is the casting principle. "Cast thy bread upon the waters: for thou shalt find it after many days" (Eccl 11:1). "And he said unto them, Cast the net on the right side of the ship, and ye shall find. They cast, therefore, and now they were not able to draw it for the

---

[78.] 2015 Blackbaud Report, Online article, accessed June 24, 2020, http://www.thenonprofittimes.com/wp-content/uploads/2015/03/Diversity-in-Giving-Study-FINAL.pdf

multitude of fishes" (Jn 21:6). The casting principle for investments involves sowing seeds in deep water. Deep water represents areas that may be unchartered. Churches that do the same thing year after year die due to stagnation. Many churches are fearful of investments because it may be unchartered territory. However, just because something is new and unchartered should not be grounds for dismissal.

The casting principle also involves long-term commitments. These investments include building a foundation for youth, young adults, and the next generation. Most of our churches historically were built to sustain the present generation with little emphasis for future generations. What do these investments look like? It is not the nature of this paper to claim which investments are best for a church body. Every church has different needs. The needs assessment of a local church should dictate the type of investments. However, all churches should invest in some type of financial plan. This may include, but not limited to, mutual funds, low-risk stocks, local municipal bonds, and endowments. Our White church brothers and sisters have historically seen the benefits of these types of investments for their churches.

It is probably fitting to speak about your local church having a 501(c)(3) status. Many granting agencies, private and public, require organizations like churches to have a 501(c)(3) status. To some churches, this sparks fears. Many of our smaller churches believe that churches are giving up their rights to the government by having a 501(c)(3) status. This is not the case. Contributors that give to churches and other nonprofit organizations are required to document their contributions. The 501(c)(3) status allows these entities to satisfy government requirements.

The casting principle also involves being obedient to the one who is giving the command. In John 21, it is Jesus who gives the orders to the disciples to cast their nets. We may question the location, the methods, and the messenger, but we should be unified in this one truth; it is Jesus giving the command. Knowing that we are obedient to Christ helps us overcome our fears.

Our overcoming the fears of investments has more to do with our faith. Jesus spoke more about finances than any other topic in the New Testament. Why? Even the Lord knew that faith is directly linked to how a person gives. Black churches invest the least. The low investment rate of the Black church may speak more about our faith. We would not admit this. However, the record speaks for itself. As a test of his faith, a Jewish ruler was asked by Jesus to invest his money in the poor (Lk 18:18–25). The ruler declined Jesus's offer. Luke records that the man was very sorrowful because he was very rich. Jesus noted the faiths of two strangers (non-Jewish). One was a Roman centurion (Mt 8:8–13) and the other a Gentile woman (Mt 15:21–28). The irony about these two situations was that the two persons exhibiting great faith were not Jews. Maybe the principle of faith with respect to our investments must be a different kind of faith. Maybe our faith is too weak because we have become conditioned. But the faith of the new generation is untested. It will do the church some good to listen to different voices for a change. Ultimately and textually, the two persons' faith matched Jesus's faith. Jesus was impressed with them because he saw himself in them. It is only when the church has Jesus's faith that the church, and especially the Black church, will overcome fear with faith.

The third aspect of investments involves the future of the Black church. Some in the church cannot see the need for investments because they are only looking at the "now." What plans have been made for the church to sustain its social relevance for the future? Whatever we do now should always point to twenty and fifty years into the future. When asked about the kingdom of God, Jesus took children in his midst and said, "Suffer little children, and forbid them not, to come unto me; for of such is the kingdom of heaven" (Mt 19:14, also see Mt 18:1–3).

The Black church's future are our children. What plans do we have in place to sustain the church for them? Whatever we do now should involve the youth and young adults of the church *now*. How do we incorporate the interests of our young people with the direct mission of Christ? There is a connection. One goal could be to build a family life center. This family life center could be used for a daycare, pre-K program, afterschool program, and a senior center extension. Weekly athletics could be housed in this facility with Bible study components. The building and the various programs may qualify for certain grants provided your church has a current 501(c) (3). The family life center could contain an unlimited number of programs all specific to the needs of your church body and community.

Can the Black Church Survive This?
Service

The service of the church is to fulfill the mandate of Christ "to go and teach all nations, baptizing them in the name of the Father, and of the Son, and of the Holy Ghost: Teaching them to observe all things whatsoever I have commanded you" (Mt 28:19–20).

One reason that the Black church is losing its footing in the current culture is because we are disconnected from Jesus Christ and his greatest commission. We allow everything to go on in the church. And when the gospel is under consideration in our church settings, it is treated as any other agenda item to be discussed in length, voted on, and once again tabled. And if not tabled, it is given to the pastor to do by himself with no or little assistance from the congregation. The gospel is the primary purpose of the entire church and not the mission of one person or one particular group of the church.

First, let us be clear on what the gospel is. The gospel is the good news of Jesus's death atonement for man's sin. Thus, we are called to share the gospel of Jesus to sinners. To share in the good news of Jesus is more than lip service. Sharing the gospel is caring for others. The Gospel of Luke illustrates Jesus's care for the marginally rejected socially, economically, and religiously. Secondly, how can we communicate the gospel to every aspect of church life? When the gospel of Jesus Christ is our goal, every subgroup of the church must have that same focus.

It is because of the gospel that the church should be involved in social change. The church should have been the first to sound the alarm on police brutality of African Americans. Why? Because racism, hatred, and institutional racism denies and betrays the gospel of Jesus Christ. However, just like the White church was silent on racism in the early nineteen hundreds, so is the Black church silent on issues of police brutality and other discriminatory acts in this country.

So then what is the service of the church? The church is called to go outside of its walls to serve the community where it exists. This service is twofold. The church is called to serve those who are within its reach (current membership). However, if this is all we do, there would never be any growth. Secondly, the church is called to go outside of its reach with the gospel of Christ. How does that gospel look like? Christ's gospel is a message of forgiveness, love, caring, and restoration. In order to give the gospel, we must first live the gospel. John's gospel shows Jesus "abiding" with the believers. If the church is unwilling to abide with the people of its community, then that church will not survive. It is when we invest in our communities through our service that those communities will be attracted to us, and that is the only way Christ can draw people to himself.

What kinds of services can a church render to the community where it exists? Each church must access its own community concerning the needs. Most churches will already have people within their walls who are qualified to meet those needs. Most churches have nurses, social-psychological-related experts, teachers, and other professionals. These are valuable resources to render adequate services for any community. If we don't use the talents of our church members, others will.

Can the Black church survive this? "This" refers to the current downward trend in society that is causing the church to be irrelevant socially, economically, and spiritually. I believe the church can survive "this" if we keep Jesus and his mission as ours. I believe there is hope for the Black church if we follow Job's example. The Bible says of Job,

> And the Lord turned the captivity of Job, when he prayed for his friends: also, the Lord gave Job twice as much as he had before. Then came there unto him all his brethren, and all his sisters, and all they that had been of his acquaintance before,

and did eat bread with him in his house: and they bemoaned him, and comforted him over all the evil that the Lord had brought upon him: every man also gave him a piece of money, and everyone an earring of gold. So the Lord blessed the latter end of Job more than his beginning: for he had fourteen thousand sheep, and six thousand camels, and a thousand yoke of oxen, and a thousand she asses. He had also seven sons and three daughters. And he called the name of the first, Jemima; and the name of the second, Kezia; and the name of the third, Kerenhappuch. And in all the land were no women found so fair as the daughters of Job: and their father gave them inheritance among their brethren. After this lived Job an hundred and forty years, and saw his sons, and his sons' sons, even four generations. (Job 42:10–16)

What can we learn from Job with respect to our present condition within the Black church? First, God turned Job's situation around after he prayed for his friends. Job's friends were very critical of him. But Job prayed for them. The Black church must pray for this nation. In order for the Black church to overcome, it too must learn the prayer of forgiveness. Secondly, Job's family and friends all invested in him financially (Job 42:11). Job was ruined, but his family and friends believed that God was not through with him. They took a risk to invest in such a one. The future of the Black church will involve taking risks. If God can turn Job's situation around, I believe the Lord can turn the Black church's situation around also. Thirdly, when God turned Job's captivity around, Job honored his three daughters equally with his sons. Job names his three daughters by name. The names of the sons are not mentioned. What a high honor Job placed on his daughters. Job knew that his future and the future of his family rested not only with his sons but also his daughters. The Black church must not forget to honor the sanctity of marriage and Black motherhood. If the Black race in America is to survive and thrive, the Black church must be the leading voice of paying honor and respect to Black women. If we don't, then the world will make claim to womanhood in a humanistic and anti-biblical fashion.

Lastly, notice in Job 42:16, the writer records, "After this, Job lived a hundred and forty years." The Black church is in the midst of a "this" situation. I believe as Job, we will survive with God's help if we are adaptable, if we make the right investments, and if we make the Great Commission of Christ our main goal in the church. And then it will be said even of the church, "After this…"

Summary and Conclusions

This book represents the variable thinking of its contributors. There has been no effort to synthesize the content or in any way integrate thought and content, with one notable exception. This exception is the *church* and, in particular, the *Black church*. This notable exception is critical for the readers of this manuscript because even the Black church is not universal in thought, organization, or behavior. Regardless, however, of its multiple nature, the Black church has been at the heart of Black struggles for liberation, holistic human development, community development, and a proactive force from a secular world of racial injustice, oppression, and unequal access to the resources necessary for life.

In his book *Liberation, A Black Theology of Liberation*, James H. Cone (Cone 1970) lays out these premises. First, to preach the gospel today means confronting the world with the reality of Christian freedom. Secondly, the church not only proclaims the good news of freedom; it actively shares the good news of freedom. Thirdly, the church as a fellowship is a visible manifestation that the gospel is a reality.

One only needs to add to James Cone's three observations of the church the word *black* to distinguish it from universal vastness!

The import of this conclusion has been magnificently summarized in the words of Lerone Bennett in his book *The Challenge of Blackness* (Bennett 1972).

> Blackness is a challenge because it raises the whole question of values and because it tells us that we must rise now to the level of teaching this profoundly ignorant and profoundly sick society. In order to do that, we must create a new

rationale. We must create a new rationality, a new way of seeing, a new way of reasoning, a new way of thinking. Our thinking—and the scholarship which undergirds that thinking—is Europe centered, white centered, property, and place centered. We see now through a glass whitely, and there can be no more desperate and dangerous task than the task which faces us now of trying to see with our own eyes.

Beyond the challenges set forth by Lerone Barrett is the critical observation of Paulo Freire in his seminal book, *Pedagogy of the Oppressed* (Freire 2017). Freire posits:

While the problem of humanization has always, from an axiological point of view, been humankind's central problem, it now takes on the character of an inescapable concern. Concern for humanization leads at once to the recognition of dehumanization, not only as an ontological possibility but as an historical reality. And as an individual perceives the extent of dehumanization, he or she may ask if humanization is a viable possibility. Within history, in concrete, objective contexts, both humanization and dehumanization are possibilities for a person as an uncompleted being conscious of their incompletion.

But while both humanization and dehumanization are real alternatives, only the first is the people's vocation. This vocation is constantly negated, yet it is affirmed by that very negation.

As an extension of Freire's observations, readers are encouraged to read *The New Jim Crow* by Michelle Alexander (Alexander 2012) which gives us a twenty-first-century view of an imperfect Black freedom.

In closing, as everyone knows, America as of this publishing is in the midst of a health crisis (pandemic) paralleling the depression of 1929. The fundamental question this new reality dictates when life, as we all formerly knew it, will no longer exist is, *What role will the Black church play in the new normal of the future?* Let's have an open and honest discussion on the question.

Creigs C. Beverly, PhD
Olivia D. Beverly, PhD

REFERENCES

Alexander, Michelle. 2010, 2012. *The New Jim Crow: Mass Incarceration in the Age of Colorblindness*. New York: The New York Press.

Bennett, Lerone. 1972. *The Challenge of Blackness*, p. 67. Chicago, Illinois. Johnson Publishing Co. Inc.

Bennett, Lerone. 1972. *The Challenge of Blackness*. Johnson Publishing Co., p. 36

Billingsley, Andrew and Rodriguez, Barbara Morrison. 2007. "The Black Family in the Twenty-First Century and the Church as an Action System: A Macro Perspective." L. See (ED.), Human Behavior in the Social Environment from an African American Perspective (p. 64), Binghamton, NY: The Haworth Press

Cone, James H. 1970. *Liberation: A Black Theology of Liberation*. New York and Philadelphia: J. B. Lippincott & Co., pp 228–233.

Freire, Paulo. 2017. *Pedagogy of the Oppressed*. New York: Bloomsbury Academic, pp 43–63.

Lincoln, C. Eric. 1986. "The Black Church and Black Self-Determination." Paper read before the Association of Black Foundation Executives, April 15, 1986. Kansas City, Missouri.